DANCING
The Inner Serpent

Memoirs of a Suburban Snake Priestess

Le'ema
Kathleen Graham

www.goddesswork.com

DANCING THE INNER SERPENT
Memoirs of a Suburban Snake Priestess

A GoddessWork Book / June 2010

All rights reserved.
Copyright © 2009, 2010 by Le'ema Kathleen Graham

This book, or parts thereof, may not be reproduced in any form without permission from the publisher; exceptions are made for brief excerpts used in published reviews.

Published by
GoddessWork
www.goddesswork.com
www.snakeyoga.com

ISBN: 978-0-9800439-1-4

Printed in the United States

Cover Painting: Hrana Janto

Book Design: Eric Bobrow

Cover Design:
Hrana Janto/Sound Vision - Graphic Design Services
Eric Bobrow

Praise for *Dancing the Inner Serpent*

"Le'ema Kathleen Graham's *Dancing the Inner Serpent* reveals intimate details of how one woman gracefully integrates a life of spirit with her day-to-day responsibilities as wife and mother. Her amazing story encourages and inspires those of us still finding our way. The beauty of her dancing and flow of her writing are evidence of commitment to her craft and love for her family, which of course includes her magnificent snakes."

—Margaret Wade
Co-author of *Reclaiming Eros*

"*Dancing the Inner Serpent* is a lush, urgent Hero's Journey for women, for embodied seekers, and for dancers, in particular, who so rarely read their story this adeptly penned!"

—Dunya Dianne McPherson
Author of *Skin of Glass: Finding Spirit in the Flesh*

"When it is so important to reconstruct what it means to be a Priestess of Goddess in contemporary times, Le'ema offers a template for women to live their lives with authenticity and awaken the priestess within."

—Rev. Karen Tate, MsGS, Prs. of Isis, FOI Adepta
Author of *Sacred Places of Goddess: 108 Destinations* and
Walking an Ancient Path: Rebirthing Goddess on Planet Earth
Host of "Voices of the Sacred Feminine"

"*Dancing the Inner Serpent* is a bridge between ancient wisdom and our emerging consciousness. Ms. Graham has illuminated the path of an urban priestess, engaging the spiritual warrior and wounded healer in us all. Her courage, conviction, clarity and willingness to tell the truth supports us on our journey. The quest is at hand. This volume is full of hope, fearlessness and vision. Thank you Le'ema for lighting the way."

—Cheryl A. Malakoff, PhD., Psychologist,
Educational Director
"Realizing Your Vision Against All Odds"

"A necessary voice in these radically shifting times, our Suburban Snake Priestess Le'ema is a force of nature in a woman!"

—Jeanne Lupton
Author of *Tanka: But Then You Danced*

~ Dedication ~

I dedicate this book to Brigid, the Gaelic Goddess of my Celtic ancestors. On the day I was ordained as a Priestess, I vowed to write my book for her.

You, Oh muse of poets, You of the Holy Well and the Sacred Flame, I have honored you since I was a Catholic girl attending the Candelmas ceremonies on Imbolc, your feast day. Your presence is in my bones, urging me forward on my path.

Beautiful Brigid, may my offering please You. May these words help keep your sacred flame alive in the hearts of all women. May the waters of your sacred well be as a healing balm and nourish all who read this book.

Thank you for a lifetime of inspiration.

Le'ema Kathleen Graham, 2009

~ Acknowledgments ~

In honor and in memory of Elizabeth Shillington and Stephanie Moore: I am deeply grateful for the short but enduring contribution these two outstanding women had on my creativity and life.

To my writing companions—Christy Salo, Mary Serphos, Willie Gordon, Marvin Spector, Gina Kutchins, and Zoe Newman—for their tireless and insightful suggestions. To Lisa Alpine, Theresa Dintino and Marguerite Rigoglioso for their edits. I am very grateful to my long-term friend and writing partner, Deborah Brackman, for her belief in me. A deep gratitude goes to Hrana Janto for the exquisite painting and cover design. Thank you to JuliAnne Kaplan, the Queen of Organization, for keeping my life systematized in the chaos of creativity.

Thank you to my writing teachers, Linda Joy Myers, Leslie Kirk Campbell—and especially Clive Matson—who inspired me to follow my muse and spurred me on to completion; and to my editor, Lisa Schulman, who really listened and expertly rearranged the words to help them come alive. I also give a special thanks to Little Man, dearest friend, who gave me my first quill.

With love to my mentors, Lady Olivia Robertson, Lady Loreon Vigne, Lady Zarita Zook, Nicki Scully, and the lineage of priestesses who walk the path of Isis.

With indebtedness to each shaman, medicine man, medicine woman, Sufi master, and guru who educated me in the extraordinary realms.

I am grateful for every dance and yoga teacher who helped train my body so that it was able to become the receptive vessel of the Sacred Feminine.

Much appreciation goes to my parents who taught me how to love and care for the earth and all her creatures.

A multitude of blessings to my husband, Élan, who devoted endless hours to the formatting and design of my book and whose steadfast love and support helped me stay focused. Thanks to my tolerant and accepting son, Liam, who loves me for who I am.

And finally, to all the moms, wives, and wild women in the world who don't fit in and shatter the mold.

~ Contents ~

1	Snake Memories	3
2	Snake Secrets	9
3	Snake Vision	13
4	Snake Death	19
5	Snake Walk	27
6	Snake Bracelet	41
7	Isis ~ Egyptian Serpent Goddess	47
8	Snake Energy	53
9	Snake Lover	61
10	Snake Island	71
11	Snake Baby	79
12	Nidaba ~ Sumerian Serpent Goddess	87
13	Shamanic Snake	93
14	Kali Ma ~ Hindu Serpent Goddess	99
15	Coatlique ~ Mayan Serpent Goddess	107
16	Becoming a Snake Priestess	117
17	Medusa ~ Greek Serpent Goddess	129
18	Snake Medicine	135
19	Shopping Mall Snakes	141
20	Cleopatra's Snake Wisdom	147
21	Wadjet ~ Egyptian Serpent Goddess	155
22	A Day in the Life of a Dancing Snake Priestess	161

23	Snake Bite	171
24	Snake Venom	177
25	Full Moon Snakes	185
26	Serpent Spirals of Life and Death	197
27	Solstice Snake	205
28	Minoan Snake Priestess	211
29	Rosary Snake	221
30	Snake Sage	229
31	Athena ~ Greek Serpent Goddess	239
32	Twin Serpents	247
33	Snake Path	251
34	Return of the Snakes	257
35	Brigid ~ Ireland ~ Roots	265
36	Sekhmet ~ Egypt ~ Stars	275
	Choreographic Works	287
	Reading List	289

~ Photographs ~

1	Kathy in the desert in a tutu	7
3	Mary Standing on the Snake	17
4	Guadalupe	24
	Kathleen age 18	25
5	Dancing at University of New Mexico	39
7	Le'ema as Isis	51
8	Kathleen in the Mountains of New Mexico	61
9	Le'ema as The Lady of The Lake	68
	Le'ema and Élan dancing as Duet With Soul	69
10	Élan and Le'ema	79
11	Le'ema dancing with Nidaba while pregnant	85
15	Our Lady of Guadalupe Dance	115
16	Ananda Mayama	126
	Le'ema is ordained by Lady Loreon and Lady Olivia	127
	Lady Olivia and Élan	127
	Le'ema and Lady Loreon under the Isis Tree	128
	Snake Priestesses in front of Temple at Isis Oasis	128
17	Le'ema as Medusa	134
19	Family Photo – Fall 1998	146
20	Le'ema dancing in the ancient ways	153
21	Gypsy Dance	169
	Lamia	170
24	Shedding Your Old Skin Ceremony, October 2001	182
	Le'ema as Lamia in the Desert	183

25	Brooke Medicine Eagle with Le'ema	196
26	Ammachi with cobra	203
28	Le'ema as the Minoan Snake Priestess	220
31	Athena Dance – September 9, 2001	246
34	Le'ema as Queen of the Snakes leading the Pagan Pride Parade	263
35	Le'ema in Ireland at St. Brigid's Well	272
	Brigid's Fire Temple	272
	Lady Olivia's Huntington Castle, Clonegal	273
	New Grange	274
36	Le'ema in Egypt	286

INSIDE THIS VASE

Inside this deep blue vase are two snakes—
One connects the sun to the earth
And one flies between the stars,
    holding space and time together.
When they mate, they give birth to the whole world—
    to feathers and bones;
    ivory carvings and
    arrows made of wood and stone;
    the soft warmth of flesh;
    the ending of hunger and war;
    and the laughter of love.
You are inside, and so is the one who holds this pen.
And the mystery. The everpresent mystery.
When you want to leave the vase, just smile.
Your breath will carry you home—
    but you will have left your image
        indelibly etched
            on the inside.

©Lion Goodman   July 1992

1

Snake Memories

The dancing, dreaming, divining gifts came with me into this life. I was born a priestess. The official ordination didn't come until later. From the chrysalis of my being I had to grow into a woman before I could realize my soul's blueprint. What was hidden from my consciousness would be revealed over many years. Like the desert flower that only blooms when kissed by nourishing rains, I would have to wait to embrace my fate.

My birthplace was a sunny dry landscape, empty of vegetation except for a few cactus and tumbleweeds that would blow across the desert floor under stark blue skies during windstorms.

My true ancestors were somewhere far away on misty emerald isles. I did not know of the Druid priests and priestesses nor of the standing stone circles where they made their altars and held their rituals under full moon nights. Nothing did I know of my Celtic ancestry, only that I was brought into existence as a baby from my mother's womb in a place called El Paso—aptly named "The Pass" as I would pass through it on my way to future journeys that would sweep me away like a tumbleweed far from my starting point.

My incarnation into this body this lifetime occurred in the Year of the Water Dragon, when the sun was in the thirteenth constellation, *Ophiuchus*, also known as Serpentarius, the Serpent Holder. My mother was a young, vibrant girl of eighteen. She always told me that I danced out of her womb in one long contraction. She became pregnant with me while my father was home on leave from the Korean War. He fought in the front lines as a soldier of twenty-two until I was six months old when he was released to come home to his first born daughter.

Dad's father, Granddaddy Graham, was present during my birth. He adored and cherished me in my early years and gave me my first few ballet lessons as a gift from the tooth fairy at age seven. Granddaddy was a devout Catholic, but he was also a passionate Scorpio man who married several times and was excommunicated from the Church. That never stopped him from attending Sunday Mass. He took me to church with him when I was a wee thing in diapers.

Granddaddy told me that I would stand in the pew with one leg propped on his knee and my arm around his neck during High Mass. One Sunday morning, Granddaddy reached into his suit coat for his wallet to put money into the collection basket but instead found that one of my petite turds had rolled out of my diaper and nestled itself comfortably in his pocket. I am sure this is where my fascination for the sacred and the profane had its origins.

For eight years, my siblings and I attended the Catholic School of St. Joseph, the father and guardian of Jesus. I was one of a few *hueritas*, fair ones, in my school, which consisted mostly of working-class Mexicans. My father was a blue-collar worker for the Army at Fort Bliss, and my mom was a striving-to-be perfect fifties housewife. The oldest of four children, I knew how to cook, clean, sew, feed, and diaper babies by the time I was ten. On Sundays, my mother would take us to church while my father stayed home and worked on one of his jalopies sitting in our driveway.

I remember the smell of the candles and frankincense wafting in the air of the church, and the priests dressed in royal purple vestments with golden trim over white garments but especially the ritual act of cannibalism where we ate the body of Christ. The white wafer would partially melt on my tongue while the rest clung to the roof of my mouth, gradually dissolving through the rest of the Mass. I savored the lingering sacrament and its sweet time with me, the "young bride of Christ." This richness of the sacred imbued upon me a holiness that was more than divine. It was mine.

I pretended I was the priest giving Holy Communion to the neighborhood kids. Cotton bed sheets were my white vestments for distributing the even whiter holy sacrament of Wonder Bread to my congregation. There was Billy, the neighborhood bully, and his little brother dressed in their dirty overalls with toy pistols hanging from holsters around their hips; Nancy, with her thick eye glasses and a dirty blond pony tail; my little sister, Linda, her chestnut locks in a pixie haircut with two front teeth missing; and my baby brother, a wide-eyed preschooler coaxed from his tricycle. When my cousins would visit, my elfin congregation grew bigger, and I would feel even more omnipotent.

"In Nomine Patri, et Spiritu, et Sanctus," I would say, displaying my Latin verbiage with flair. The children's eyes squinted shut as I placed the white gooey substance on outstretched tongues protruding from expectant faces. The communion circles were made with a cookie cutter pressed into the centers of soft bread slices. I prayed over them fervently during my makeshift Mass while holding a broomstick by my side as my staff.

Would Jesus be proud of me? Sister Mary Pious, with her bulldog jowls and her southern accent, certainly wasn't. She told me, "You are an impudent brat," when I refused to answer a Catechism question that I deemed beneath my intelligence.

Later on, I thought that maybe someday I would take vows as a nun and be like my seventh grade teacher, Sister Anne Marie. She allowed me to read *The Scarlet Letter*. But I had to give an oral book report because it was not approved for a seventh grade Catholic girl. I read eagerly about Hester Prynne, a Puritan woman who becomes pregnant out of wedlock by a minister. Like Hester, my path was not to be one of celibacy, but rather of one who serves through the passion, love, pleasure, and joy of being fully in the body. The Goddess had something else in store for me.

Kathy in the desert in a tutu

2

Snake Secrets

The house on La Luz Street was a house of secrets. The small brick dwelling sat on a short block across from an elementary school in El Paso. It belonged to my maternal grandparents. We visited them often.

As I approached the concrete steps to the large porch, nausea would well up inside me. My five-year-old heart would start to pound as though I had run around the block. The odors of cigarettes, coffee, vinegar, and chewing tobacco assaulted my nostrils at the door. The sunlight disappeared the minute I walked into the house. It wasn't dark inside that house on La Luz Street, and yet there was a strange darkness that existed within its walls. It was a small house, too small, with not enough air to breathe. The living room was dirty, cluttered with ashtrays, coffee-stained mugs, and Coke bottles half-filled with my grandfather's chewing tobacco spittle. I had to hold my breath to keep out those bad smells that hung around like hungry ghosts ready to devour me. It would only make it worse if I were to follow my impulse and vomit.

Uncle Melvin, our Great Uncle, was my grandmother's brother. A crusty old man who stank to high heaven, Melvin was a deaf-mute who never learned to read lips or speak with American Sign Language. It seemed impossible to communicate with him. He would make guttural sounds whenever I sat on his lap. I didn't know that what was happening was wrong. His hands were in my underpants. It didn't feel right, but it felt good in a wrong sort of way.

It was the beginning of the shame and anger and dread that distorted my childhood.

Many years later as a young adult, I learned American Sign Language and taught hearing impaired children. Communicating to the deaf and mute through a language that used my hands gave me a voice that I never had as a child. Children don't have words to explain reptilian brain emotions, those "love gone wrong" feelings.

Uncle Melvin was not the only sexual predator in the house on La Luz Street. My grandmother's son, Buford, was young enough to be an older brother to me but old enough to know better. I soon learned I couldn't trust the adults caring for me. The betrayals that reoccurred were in my child's mind—normal. Normal seemed to be the pit of terror that lived inside my stomach each time I would enter that house on La Luz Street.

My mother said she could never understand why I kept such a cold distance from her mother. But my grandmother protected and spoiled Buford rotten. He never worked or went to school. He just hung around smoking and drinking and eyeing the "blonde bombshell" fold out pin-up girls in his girlie magazines.

I wondered why they were always smiling and how their breasts grew so large. Maybe that was why the models were so happy. I wanted to be happy like them. As a teen angel, I read movie star magazines and fancied buying the special creams or gizmos that were advertised to be mailed in discreet, brown paper packages because I wanted the happiness of big bosoms. Thankfully, mine stayed just the right proportion for my body.

Pictures of naked ladies hung everywhere in the urine-stenched den of a back porch that was my uncle's bedroom. It seemed like Buford was always in bed half-naked with the bed sheets twisted around him in some tormented fashion.

My little sister, Linda, shared my fear of him. Often we hid in the solitary closet in the house, a deep and narrow space where we held each other and shook, our teeth chattering a twin tongue of terror.

My mother always treated Linda and I like we were Irish twins. She sewed matching outfits for us in different colors. Mine had blue and white polka dots, and my sister's had pink and white polka dots. But we didn't look at all like twins. Linda had chestnut hair and soft brown eyes, and I was a tow-headed blondie with blue eyes.

Years later, when my memories resurfaced, I told my mom what had happened to me in that house on La Luz Street.

"Oh, honey, I wish you had been able to tell me then," she said. "I caught Uncle Melvin with his hand in Linda's diapers when she was two years old."

We always thought Linda was shy, but now, looking back, I see that she must have been terrorized, too. Timidity was her only protection.

When my sister and I were told to play in the backyard, we had to go through Buford's room.

"Okay," I would say to Linda, "You go first."

"No, you go first," she whispered, her eyes glued to the floor. We held our noses and covered our eyes. To get past the sleeping ogre, we ran on tiptoes without breathing or seeing.

On a few occasions when my sister was not with me, my uncle caught me. Somehow, he coaxed me into his bed. As his big hand pressed on the back of my small neck, everything began to go black. I felt as if I was going to suffocate. The pain was almost unbearable—this pain he called love that I was supposed to keep secret.

One day, after such an incident, I wanted my pain to be visible. Filled with nauseous shame, I escaped into the bathroom and climbed up onto the big old-fashioned toilet and then up to the pedestal sink, the cold white porcelain chilling my little bird bones. In the medicine cabinet was a package of razor blades. I carefully unwrapped two of them. Holding one in each hand, I jumped down off the sink and squeezed hard until I felt their fang sharp blades cut deeply into the palms of my tiny hands. It was a good, painful pleasure, one that would make the wounds of my assault visible to the adults in charge. I opened my palms to watch the blood spurt out.

See, I have wounds like Jesus, I thought. My stigmata. My sacred wounds that came from the pain of loving. Isn't that what happened to Jesus?

When I look at my hands now, I see the letter M in each palm along with a scar. Mary Magdalen, Mother Mary, Marilyn Monroe, did they have the initials M M in the palms of their hands too? Did they love Jesus the way I did? Maybe this was the mark of a secret priestesshood of the scarlet wound. The wound of love.

3

Snake Vision

> Human eye sees far
> yet into its true essence
> it is but blind
>
> —Le'ema

My first Haiku was written as a pre-adolescent. My body was little, with breasts smaller than all my classmates. But I was growing swiftly into my essence as a woman.

I especially adored the Virgin Mary and would spend hours staring at her statues and saying Hail Mary's on my rosary beads. While fervently saying my prayers one day, I gazed up at an alabaster statue of Mother Mary standing on the world with the serpent at her feet and had my first vision. The snake came to life and smiled at me as if it could speak. When I looked back up at Mary, she winked at me and whispered, "SSSshhh! Now, you know my secret." Somehow I knew that she was not stomping out evil or killing the serpent as the Church had taught. They were friends.

Perhaps I was seeing that the snake was Mary's familiar or the shaman's totem. All great avatars have their animal totems. Lord Shiva rides a bull, Saraswati floats on swans, Jesus rides a donkey, and Mary stands on her serpent. To me, the serpent was giving her energy, wisdom, and joy. I was young and precocious, but that day, I felt wise beyond my years. I vowed to keep Mary's secret, for I knew if I spoke of this, it could mean trouble.

Later that year, my grandfather died of heart failure. I was dismayed that his funeral was not held in our parish. How could the Church refuse one of its most devout members who, in my humble, child opinion, deserved to have prayers said over his dead body to help his journey onto the other realms? I took it upon myself to lead everyone in saying the rosary aloud at his memorial service. In retrospect, it was the first time I officiated a service as a priestess. I was a flower cracking through the Church concrete.

The year was 1964, when Ed White stepped out of an orbiting US Gemini spacecraft to become the first American to walk in space. My family and I watched the television footage of that monumental event. Afterwards, I slipped out into the backyard in my plaid flannel pajamas to gaze up at the nearly full moon. "Come to me, my child," beckoned the Lady.

She claimed me as her own Moon Maiden, this Moon Mother, my moon. As much as I was intrigued by the astronaut's space walk, I felt envious of his cosmic voyage. Why him? The Moon Mother doesn't want him; she wants me. I can hear her calling me. Her moonbeams streamed forth, lighting my path in a black night sky.

Mom hollered, "Come to bed."

Reluctantly, I left my moon watching, came inside, and crawled under the covers. In my dreams, the moon became a giant egg. It cracked open and thousands of luminous serpents came spinning down. Two swam toward me, entering through my belly button and spiraling inside me, coiled tightly around hundreds of tiny snake eggs on each side of my womb. Some circled around me, weaving a big basket that carried me out to sea. I felt wetness between my legs that woke me.

I sat up in the bed and gasped. Both my hands were covered in blood, every finger stained red like the hennaed hands of a classical Indian temple dancer. I felt weird and wonderful at the same time. When my mother saw this, she exclaimed, "You're a woman now."

The thought of a Kotex pad was absurd to me. The white bulging thing stuck between my thighs and held in place with an elastic band strapped around my waist felt clunky. It was an insult. I wanted to go back to the dream, to find the meaning of those mysterious serpents. Snake dreams still come to me today. Later, I would remember this. It wasn't until menopause that I understood my first blood was an initiation, and that the dream was not only my personal space voyage to the moon but also a voyage into personal power.

My periods were never easy throughout my fertile years. Plagued by cramping, heavy bleeding, mood swings, and intense psychic awareness, I thought at times I should die. How could I have known that the pre-moon time of sexual abuse would have imprinted such a negative experience on my womanliness? I had completely shut out those memories until my symptoms were so bad, they forced me into serious inquiry and therapy. After forty-one years of menstrual misery, I had my last period at Brigid's Holy Well on the island of my ancestors. Menopause was a celebration for me of the end of trauma that had been stored in my womb and reactivated during my menses all those cycles.

And now that I am holding my wise moon blood within, I can tell these stories. Stories of death, stories of birth, stories of life. With the Lady and Her Snakes as a living presence in my innermost being, I knew I would always find guidance. My life as a Snake Priestess began when I was twelve, the night the first American astronaut stepped out into space. The night I became a womb one.

Snake Vision

Mary Standing on the Snake

4

Snake Death

After the childhood protection of Catholic grade school, I entered the teenage chaos of a public high school in the fall following the San Francisco Summer of Love. Later in my freshman year, Bobby Kennedy and Martin Luther King were assassinated. The world around me seemed to unravel as if on the verge of apocalypse.

Clinging to familiar territory, I sang in the choir all four years and studied drama and literature. I dated my altar boy sweetheart through high school, and in the Summer of 1969, while Woodstock was making history in upstate New York, I was making love for the first time in the back seat of a VW bug at the drive-in movie theater in El Paso after watching Franco Zeffirelli's version of *Romeo and Juliet*.

My virginal innocence, and much more, was lost in my senior year when my sibling rival, Linda, just sweet sixteen, breathed her last breath. I received the pass to the nurse's office during drama that November afternoon. At the end of the long corridor, I could see my favorite aunt walking back and forth. Her nervous pacing told me something was wrong. A passing cloud darkened the hallway where only moments before the sun had streamed through the wall of windows. I stood there, watching, as my whole world became a blur. In slow motion, my aunt reached out and gathered me in her arms. She enveloped me, rocking me back and forth, back and forth.

"She's dead," she whispered in a cracking voice. "Your sister, Linda, is dead."

My throat held tight a scream that would never be heard. I wanted to run. Hide.

The sun never came back out that day.

Linda, like St. Theresa the Little Flower, had been diagnosed with epilepsy, the divine falling sickness, when she was twelve. My parents spent several years trying every medication possible to get her seizures under control. Linda was in and out of the hospital, but nothing seemed to work. That morning she had an attack at home and drowned. My mother found her. Floating face down in the bathtub. Silent. The only sign of a struggle were the crumpled shower curtains she had pulled down upon her.

Linda had been a fine artist. A few days before her death, I watched as she painted a forest scene with a young nude woman in the middle of the trees. She kept painting it darker and darker with browns and ochres. The words, *This painting has a foreboding sense of death*, kept echoing inside my head.

I had no idea of my psychic abilities at the time, and the premonition confused me. Had my dreadful thoughts caused her death? It took several years for me to work through an ambiguous sense of guilt. Suffering and loss became a path of initiation, a layer of complexity added to my being.

Soon after her death, I heard through the grapevine that my boyfriend was seeing someone else. I called him on his deception and ended the relationship. It was yet another loss.

During this time, my father took to drinking heavily. Late one night, there was a pounding on our front door. I opened it to find my father draped over a stranger's arms like a lifeless Jesus taken down from the Cross. A sickly sweet smell leaked from his pores. My heart clenched into a tight fist.

My mother pushed past me. "Go back to bed, Kathy!" she commanded.

Certain he was dead, I cried myself to sleep that night. No one came to tell me otherwise.

The next morning, I shuffled out of my room to see my dad in the kitchen, making coffee. My mom stood before an open fridge.

"We're out of milk," she said.

I turned around and left.

It was the beginning of a loneliness that would never end. I thought that everyone I loved, as well as God the Father, had abandoned me. Everything around me was dreary; I felt lost as if I was cursed. Was this what Jesus must have felt when he cried out, "My God, my God, why hast Thou forsaken me?"

Was I not worthy of the Father's love?

The shamed part of me believed that I had deserved all of this. I don't know how many times I must have gone to confession, just to confess my unworthiness.

Father Sullivan, a jolly young man and an anchor of kindness, humility, and humor was my confessor. He brought new music into the church with his guitar and a sonorous tenor voice. I sought refuge in the comfort of his loving presence, modeling myself after him and hoping to find my own direction through music. The power of the voice to uplift and heal has always touched me.

Night after night in my room, steeping in the dark space of a lonely sacred heart, I built secret shrines to the gods of music as I listened to their voices: Joan Baez, James Taylor, Joni Mitchell, and Leonard Cohen. The existential aloneness of death and birth that all great poets attempt to define spoke to the very depths of my soul.

Father Sullivan gave me the usual ten Hail Mary's to say. The prayer was intended as penance, but it became my consolation. Ever since, it has been a contemplative practice.

> Hail Mary, Full of Grace,
> The Lord is with Thee.
> Blessed Art Thou among women
> And blessed is the fruit of Thy womb,
> Jesus.
> Holy Mary, Mother of God,
> Pray for us sinners,
> Now and at the hour of our death,
> Amen.

That was when I began praying harder than ever to Our Lady. And that was when Mary became more potent to me than Jesus. Why? Because I realized she was the Mother of God. Wouldn't the Mother of God be more powerful than God? And who was God's mother? The Goddess. She was the Mother of the Universe who could take on many forms.

On the afternoon of my eighteenth birthday, December 9, 1970, one month after my sister's death, I walked into St. Joseph's to make my usual devotion to Mary. No one was there. This time, instead of going straight to the front of the church to the life-size statues of Jesus next to Mary standing on her serpent, I ducked into the back vestibule. There, underneath the tiled mosaic image of Our Lady of Guadalupe, I knelt and lit three candles—one for myself, one for my sister, and one for my mother. Closing my eyes, I bowed my head in reverence. Lost in quiet solitude, time seemed to stretch into eternity, and space opened into a vast realm. When I opened my eyes, Guadalupe shone from within like a thousand suns behind the clouds. The whole church seemed to glow from the light of the Goddess.

Guadalupe, Lady of Mercy, Lady of Light, Queen of Roses. Guadalupe was everywhere in that West Texas town of El Paso. She was a patron saint of the poor, of the forgotten, of the dispossessed, and of prisoners. She was the one whom Mexican boys had tattooed on their bodies. The Mother of All, Brown Madonna for the Americas, was the re-emergence of Maria Magdalena on this continent. The starry mantle of Guadalupe has always reminded me of my roots and the tribal connection I feel to the earth—the fertile mystery mistress—the Goddess incarnate. I never seemed to notice that she was brown, and I was white. She was still *mí Madré*, my Mother, and I her daughter. She was Goddess to me, and I, her priestess to be.

Guadalupe

Kathleen age 18

5

Snake Walk

when that girl was walking there...
in the desert
she wore only the lightness
of her own skin
which the sun would not touch
because it needed her
each five a.m.
to reach up her arms and
let them telescope section by section
      to that great furnace
           in the sky

she one day played
as desert girls do
with a diamondback   slinging
it around her body pretending it clothed her
      a bikini
      a stole
      a brown and crackling belt
           that this day reached down from her waist
           and fastened its teeth on the soft flesh (dry skin)
           between her thighs
                and let go to seep venom
                      onto the grayness under her feet

and she bled...
she bled for five days
    and was unable to light the sun
        because her arms were wrapped around her belly

when that girl stopped bleeding
she played again
in the desert
and was dancing with the shadow
of an eight foot saguaro
    oh the grace with
    which she spun
    herself
    among its furry arms
and the cactus shook loose a thorn
with a wink of its great blossom
loosened the prick and
threw it beneath that girl
    who knelt and cried
    who removed the thorn
    with her teeth
    who placed a hand upon her heart
        to find a breast had grown
            pear shaped surprise

who spent the next day
in a cave
trying to grow another
for she felt odd there
    with the animals her friends
        crows
        scorpions
        optimistic little rats
            watching her try to balance
                a lopsided body
and that girl there
in her cave
in her unlit cool cave
    felt the right side become
        a breast

Snake Walk

so toward the end of day
she went out and could
walk with ease
    shoulders slightly
    back with the weight

she walked
until she passed
a form some sea
had left to thrash
its way about the
desert in search of
water
    heavy form
    fish form
    fins sprinkled with sand
and she leaned to spit in its
creaking mouth
to see its eyes open
popping with gratitude
    to rise again and feel for her
        first time thirsty

she left the desert...
left for a place with pipelines and wells
hitched rides with
men in weed scratched pick-ups
    who never mentioned
    her nakedness
    because she still wore a
        glittering diamondback around
        her waist

that girl lives now
in an apartment
with a supply of water to keep her
    and alone because
    all her years of

>   reaching the sun
>   have left her too tall
>   for many men
>
> she watches the sunrise
> with only a twinge
> of longing
> wondering if anybody
> will ever fire it as she did
>   on time
>   thoroughly fired when
>   she was there but
>   now it shows an occasional
>   dark spot
>   she wouldn't have overlooked
>
> and she bides her time
> until the time she climbs
> in the coolness of night
>   because she is
>   changed
>   climbs surely
>   with her greatwomanbody
>   to ride the moon
>
>   —Author Unkown

Nuevo Mexico—Tierra del Encanto, New Mexico, the Land of Enchantment, will always be my spirit home here on Earth.

When I was a young child, my parents built a summer cabin at Elephant Butte, New Mexico. The desert became my playground. The rocks and dirt of the land were my teachers, as were the creepy crawlies. My sister and I made pet friends with lizards, but they would escape just as quickly as we caught them, leaving us with only their tails in our fingertips as they scurried off to grow new ones.

I grew my own lizard tail when I walked on sharp, hot rocks with bare feet in the blazing sun and felt my root moving deep down through the layers of sand and crystals and magma into the center of the earth.

I was fearless in those days, but my mother wasn't.

"Take a stick when you go on that hike," she demanded, arms waving in the air. She resembled a fire and brimstone evangelist preaching the wrath of the Apocalypse. "And beat the bushes with it before you pass by."

"But I love snakes, Mom."

"You can never be too careful."

"You are so paranoid," I sneered as I picked up a walking stick. I spit at her. "SSS…Maybe a snake will bite me!" I slammed the door and stalked out into the desert.

One summer, my family went on a camping trip in the Gila Wilderness of New Mexico. On a narrow trail called the Cat Walk, my father killed a diamondback rattler with a shovel and brought the rattles back to show us. My mind was captivated at the thought of meeting that exotic diamondback. Yet, sadness overcame me when my father jiggled the rattles in my face.

"Would ya take a look at this. It sure was a big son-of-a-bitch!" he bragged.

I felt cheated for not being able to see the whole snake and wondered what Dad did with its body. I thought back to my vision with Our Lady gently gliding on her serpent. And then I thought about those macho cowboys who wore rattlesnake belts around their waists with brass Lone Star State buckles and matching rattlesnake boots for kicking the shit out of someone.

Moccasins were preferable to boots for me, and I have always worn them. I was the Indian maiden who refused to ever play cowboy. It was during that same trip when we visited the Gila Cliff dwellings outside of Silver City that I remembered a lifetime being one of those indigenous people long ago, foraging for food in the forest, grinding corn on a stone slab, and hunting with a bow and arrow.

Earlier, when I was a tow-headed six year old, during a visit to Taos Pueblo, a tribal elder came over to me and placed his hands upon my head. I can still hear his calm voice, see his wise face, and feel the power that came through those brown, cracked hands as they touched my wispy white locks.

"This child has a special destiny," he told my parents.

*   *   *

Darren, a debonair, Clark Gable look-alike, was born and bred in New Mexico. We met after he returned from active duty in the Army. I was a naïve nineteen year old, working as a secretary at the Chevrolet dealership in El Paso. After a summer romance, we moved to Albuquerque to begin a more adventurous life than I had previously known. My VW Bug was stuffed to over-flowing as I followed behind his pick-up truck across the flatlands of Texas up to the high desert mountains of my mystical New Mexico.

When we first started dating, he told me that his background in metaphysics and parapsychology enabled him to communicate with the dead. One night, I asked him if he would contact Linda's spirit. Obliging, he sat with palms facing up on his lap in a straight-backed chair in the middle of my parents' living room. In the dim light, I waited anxiously on the couch as he entered a trance state.

His eyelids fluttered when he made the connection, and then he said, "Linda has a message for you. She says, 'Sis, do not be sad for me, I am happy. It is you who has the harder fate and the greater destiny…"

Darren's ability to bring her back amazed me, and I fell hard for his spiritual sensitivity. It was this same sensitivity that later took him down a path of destruction. He used cigarettes, coffee, alcohol—every substance available—to numb his emotions.

We joined in wedlock when I was twenty on the Mescalero Apache Indian Reservation in a Cathedral-style church built from the peach-colored flagstone so prevalent in the southwest. Bats flew around the belfry the evening of our sunset wedding. The bat, a totem animal to shamans, is considered to be the medicine of death and rebirth. Was the shaman's death and rebirth inherent in this union? Of course, I couldn't have known then that our relationship, encapsulating both glory and tragedy, would lift me from the confines of a shattered childhood glued together by Catholicism and deliver me on an unusual path of renewal.

Getting me out of Texas was the best thing Darren ever did for me. The Rio Grande River led me farther north to discover the land where I had spent the summers of my youth. We lived a life immersed in Native American culture that nurtured my spirit as a homecoming to ancient roots. We spent many languorous hours visiting pueblos, camping in the mountains, soaking in hot springs, hiking among ruins, and participating in Pow Wows and ceremonies. We had Navaho, Apache, and Pueblo Indian friends. Fry bread and red chili became a staple in our diet.

Together, we partook of hallucinogenic plants. Marijuana, magic mushrooms, and peyote were medicine teachers. Marijuana expanded my mind and taught me how to mellow out and listen within. Mushrooms opened my vision to the moving matrix of all living things. And Grandfather Peyote opened my heart to the oneness and unity inherent among all people. The ingestion of these plants with their mind-altering abilities became a sacrament to me. I thought Darren was experiencing the same kind of awakening. But the longer I was with him, the more I saw that he was just getting high. The higher the better. His substance-abuse problem was obvious, but I couldn't acknowledge it.

My relationship with Darren was fleeting, immature even, but it helped me shed a skin on my journey of the snake. I needed to experience the world around me, and Darren, with his eccentric nature, sanctioned my explorations. We enjoyed the freedom of sunbathing and swimming nude, having other lovers and dancing at wild parties. Our open marriage allowed me to release not only my inhibitions, but also the layers of shame and guilt that had been ingrained in me from the Church's conservative dogma. I was no longer a Catholic in chains.

One time, at his prompting, I took a job as a stripper at the Magic Pyramid Adult Theatre on Central Avenue in Albuquerque. Between shows, a girlfriend and I, layered in pastel-colored silken veils, took turns removing our garments down to our G-strings while prancing around the stage under black lights to Pink Floyd music. Later, I would learn that an *ecdysiast* is a humorous description for a performer of striptease. And fittingly, the meaning of the term *ecdysis* is the regular molting of an outer layer by reptiles. The gig only lasted two weeks during the fall as it was entertainment for cowboys who were in town for the New Mexico State Fair, but the exhilaration, as well as the liberation I felt, brought me a step closer to my calling as a dancer.

One could say it was our sex, drugs, and rock-n-roll era. My mother said, "The worst thing Darren did for you was get you into all that nekked stuff." Yet, I believed my experiences with him opened a doorway to the divine that was beyond the parameters of Church.

Once, on a backpacking trip, we ran into a man on the trail, boasting about his kill of a diamondback rattlesnake. He possessed not only the rattles but also the skin.

Darren asked, "What did you do with the snake?"

The fellow proudly pointed us in the direction of his slaughter. We hiked back to the place where it had been left dismembered on the trail. We took it back to our camp and roasted it over an open fire. It was delicious, with the consistency of fish and the flavor of chicken. Eating rattlesnake was an act of ingesting the manna of serpent. This was a new kind of communion for me.

When a shaman eats a totem animal, it is said that the animal is a generous giver of bounty. Rattlesnake made a temple in my belly that day. I didn't know snake would become my totem then, but I believe that because I had empathy for this maligned creature of the reptile kingdom, it chose me to be a conduit for its healing power. In the years that followed, I would learn much about healing myself.

Darren and I attended the University of New Mexico in Albuquerque. After taking a couple of dance classes as electives, my ballet teacher called me aside one day and said, "Kathleen darling, you have the talent to train as a professional dancer." Finally, I could open the gift of my heart's yearning.

My teacher was the first one to call me by my birth name, Kathleen. The name, meaning Noble One, gave me dignity. I felt a newfound sense of self-esteem that I had never before experienced. It was as if she was saying, "You are Kathleen Ann Graham. You have the potential to be a great dancer."

I did grow into the fullness of my potential but not as a ballerina. My dancing journey took me on the circuitous route of exploring dance as a healing path. And my name enabled me to become the dancer I am today.

Although my father named me after the Irish song, "I'll Take You Home Again, Kathleen," he never once called me by my birth name. As a young dancer, I begged to be called Kathleen by my parents, to no avail. To this day, they call me Kathy. They don't realize they are speaking to the ghost of a childhood past.

Through dance, I felt beautiful. My parents never told me that I had an attractive body or that I was even good looking. I had always felt embarrassed by my boyish figure and small breasts. Dance became my healing art. It was the doorway to the sacred for me. Ecstatic states were experienced simply by doing a ballet *barre*. Daily religious vows of *pliés* and *tendus* became my spiritual practice.

My love of dance had begun when Granddaddy Graham paid for my first ballet lessons. Sadly, he was unable to continue financing my artistic pursuits, and my parents, believing the gain from a Catholic education was of greater benefit to me than the pedagogy of ballet, refused my constant requests to study at the local dance academy.

I drooled over the ballets my mother occasionally took me to as a child and looked on enviously at my friends whose parents could afford lessons. After taking the bus from school, I'd stop by the ballet studio on my way home to watch other children dance. In my fantasy world, I was the prima ballerina. With the help of library books, I learned my French commands and practiced the corresponding feet, leg, torso, and arm positions at home in front of a mirror. Mom's Tupperware tumblers became my first toe shoes when I stuck them on my feet and clunked around. This was how I taught myself to stretch tall through the whole body and balance on the tip of my toes.

When my college professor put me *en pointe* in a modern ballet after only six months of training, my life as a dancer was set in motion. My potential had been waiting to be fostered. Like Sleeping Beauty, the budding young dancer in me, which had lain dormant all those years, was at last awakened.

Respect for my body as the temple of the spirit guided me to stop smoking and become a vegetarian. As I grew stronger in my dedication to the dance, I watched in disbelief as my husband grew weaker from his addictions to substances and alcohol. The bar bill from his frequent all-nighters cost almost as much as our rent each month. I couldn't tolerate it when I'd wake up in the mornings to find Darren unconscious in the bed next to me, gagging on his vomit.

Although we were married for six years, I should have known by our first anniversary that it wouldn't last. During dinner in Lamy, New Mexico, he sprayed champagne down the front of my blouse.

"Sorry, oh God, I am so sorry," he slobbered. I sat there, drenched, trying to laugh it off. The humiliation, one of many, was an ending at the beginning of what was supposed to be happily ever after.

One month later, while walking in the mountains, a green garter snake crossed my path. Instinctively, I picked up the thin, slithery creature about two feet in length and put it inside my purple cotton sweatshirt. It was the first time I had ever handled a snake, and a small miracle occurred. It seemed the creature wanted to make a connection with me. The sultry feel of the smooth serpent against my thin skin and small breasts gave rise to an erotic, rebellious impulse inside me. A feeling of sexual dignity and prowess crept into my sinews, stirring me into a state of euphoria. A story as old as time was whispered on my heart as the green snake lay upon my chest. It wasn't told in words, but in the language of *SSS*...Serpent. The snake encouraged me to trust my instincts and embrace change.

After my conversation with the snake, I knew I had to divorce Darren. I would take a bite into the apple of the unknown and like Eve risk losing what looked like paradise on the outside to find the knowledge of heaven within.

Sometimes I wish I had never read the works of Henry David Thoreau, Ralph Waldo Emerson, and Anais Nin. Whether I knew it then or not, they must have influenced that "dance to the beat of your own drummer" tune inside me that I follow like clock work. The spirit of rugged individuality was etched on my psyche forever in the words of these writers.

What we are taught to believe as truth and what we come to know as truth are often worlds apart. Had I been born into a different era, I could have been accused of being a heretic. I might have been burned at the stake. But the snake told me a truth about myself that day in the woods that was like a divine revelation to a saint—though my fascination was that of a sinner.

With snake power lurking in my creative unconscious, I made the solo *'when that girl was walking there in the desert...'* imagining dancing with that mysterious diamondback. Both the innocent skin of my youth and the protective skin I had grown through a marriage to an alcoholic husband were shed when I divorced Darren.

Dancing at University of New Mexico

6

Snake Bracelet

One month later, after graduating from the University of New Mexico with honors, I moved to Oahu to begin work on a Masters degree in dance. The Hawaiian Islands were the opposite of the desert mountains of New Mexico—a place where winters never came, and the world was wet and lush. It also took me far away from Darren.

Mornings were dedicated to ballet lessons. In the afternoons, to earn a living, I modeled nude for artists. Weekends were spent boogie boarding and body surfing at Waikiki beach. I bicycled everywhere and still had energy to burn. I sought out many lovers, hoping to fill the void left by my failed marriage. Within a short period of time, keeping up with the fast pace of Honolulu became an irritation. Even the fragrant, exotic flowers overwhelmed my senses. My nervous system missed the zen-like quality of New Mexico, of brown and mud.

In the spring of 1980, as part of the Masters curriculum, I performed in my first—and last—classical ballet, *La Bayadère*. That same year, the accomplished Russian ballerina, Nathalia Makarova, who had defected to the United States, restaged this famous romantic classic for New York's American Ballet Theatre.

A review in the New Yorker said, "Ballets passed down the generations like legends acquire a patina of ritualism, but *La Bayadère* is a ritual, a poem about dancing and memory and time."

Choreographed in 1877 by Marius Petipa, the renowned ballet master of St. Petersburg, the story follows Nikiya, an Indian temple dancer, a *bayadère*. In the end, she is killed by the bite of a poisonous serpent hidden in a basket of fruit given to her by the jealous Rajah.

It was with great pride that I played my tiny part in this historical ballet moment on the tiny Hawaiian island. As one of the corps de ballet, I joined in the monumental opening processional with thirty-two dancers. My childhood dream of being a ballerina reached fruition while dancing that languorous *arabesque penchée* sequence, costumed in a white gossamer tutu *en pointe*.

Later, as my body went through the motions of beautifully executed ballet technique in class, I found to my bewilderment that I had reached a plateau. Striving for perfection in form didn't give me the same juice it once had. A submerged longing for a spiritual teacher began to bubble up. At the same time, my love of modern dance choreography with a personal context propelled me on to a new quest—to dance the spirit in the body. The distinguished modern dancers Martha Graham, José Limón, and Doris Humphrey were great inspirations to me. Variations in movement, beyond the exhausting, precise world of the ballet, begged for expression and soon came the realization that I didn't fit in. I was a hippie with pit hair, not a clean-shaven, well-plucked ballerina. I would grow into the fullness of my potential—but not as a ballerina. My dancing journey was to take me on a circuitous route of exploring the dance as a healing path.

While island hopping on the Big Island of Hawaii, I fell in love with a man from New Mexico and moved back to Albuquerque to be with him. Our relationship never worked out.

However, we were introduced to a Sufi master together, and in truth, I had followed my heart back to New Mexico to be with this teacher, not that man.

The Sufi master helped me find a path to a richer embodiment of spirit through movement. He taught meditation and Middle Eastern dance. Every summer for several years, I lived in my tipi on the land of that Sufi community nestled in the Manzano Mountains. I followed my gypsy spirit. Like the girl in the poem, I lived in the desert for many months and "hitched rides with men in weed-scratched pick-ups who never mentioned my nakedness because I still wore a glittering diamondback around my waist."

*   *   *

It was during this wandering phase that I met Martin. One minute we were sitting on the couch watching TV, and the next, we were on the floor fucking. Martin was one of those men that women are told to avoid. He was not particularly handsome, just a sexy blend of Italian, African, and Native American heritages. He wore a gold hoop in his left earlobe, reminding me of the passionate nomad in D.H. Lawrence's story, *The Virgin and the Gypsy*. My neighbor told me he thought Martin looked like the manipulative and mesmerizing Russian rake, Rasputin. Martin liked the comparison when I told him. It elicited a throaty chuckle.

He was not much of a conversationalist. I suppose that was part of the attraction. I didn't have to talk to him. Just the magnetic, biological pull to connect with his body was enough. His swarthy skin, musky smell, and long, silky black hair drew me to him. And his lips, big and fleshy, gave the wettest kisses I had ever received. He was a luscious lover.

At twenty-seven years old, I was ripe enough for a man like him. Martin was the epitome of the Rolling Stones' adage, "You can't always get what you want, but if you try sometimes well you just might find you get what you need." I needed for my passion to be met. Thus far, a marriage and multiple lovers had never been able to touch that smoldering ember deep inside me. Through him, my wanton woman energy found expression. Martin ignited me into flame. He often teased that I might spontaneously combust someday.

With variations in love play that I had never experienced, he spun me into his seductive web. And caught by the spider, I allowed myself to be devoured over and over again.

Martin was most articulate with his hands. His hands could repair cars, build houses, lay masonry, bake bread, play piano, make love, design and create jewelry. Martin wore several bracelets that he had made on his right arm, and I was curious about them.

One afternoon, while sitting in his beat-up, blue Toyota jeep in the Sandia Mountains during a snowstorm, he told me how he had become a jewelry maker. He explained that his hands could feel the piece inside the metal begging to take shape, how he held the silver until it spoke to him of what it wanted to become. A pair of earrings? A necklace? A bracelet? In certain cultures, he said that a sign of a man's wealth was indicated by how many bracelets his woman wore. Unbeknownst to either of us, it was a bracelet that became the symbol of the path I would embark upon years later.

Uncoiling a double-headed, silver snake bracelet from his arm, Martin reached out and took my hand, placing it around my tiny wrist. He squeezed the bracelet closed and said, "This snake is for you."

A shiver went up my spine. I thanked him and told him how striking it was. I told him that it made me feel sexy in an artistic sort of way. I felt privileged to be his woman, or one of them anyway. And then, I crawled onto his lap and kissed him, flicking my tongue like a snake inside his open mouth and wriggling my hips in figure eight motions on top of him.

"Sssooo," I crooned, "can we play with your big snake now?"

We made our own fire that winter evening as the snow fell softly around us.

With Martin, I learned the secrets of the *Kamasutra*, an ancient Sanskrit text giving rules for sensual pleasure, love, and marriage in accordance with Hindu law. Memories of a lifetime as a *tantrika* and a *bayadère* awakened. Desire bred desire. It was an archetypal incestuous urge that Martin satisfied; one that Carl Jung termed, "the Electra complex," a daughter's unconscious libidinal desire for her father. And it was one of the worst relationships of my life, especially since he was so much like my father. Nevertheless, this man helped shape my destiny as a Snake Priestess.

Martin was born on the same day as my dad, so it seemed like some sort of omen that we ended up together. Like my father, Martin was uncommunicative. He never said he loved me. When he did try to talk to me, it was often with some form of teasing or criticism bereft of tenderness. But in bed, our bodies spoke the same language.

It was a sexual odyssey that stopped at the door to the heart. Mine was open, ready. His was locked shut. I fell in love. He fell in lust. My body was freed, but my heart remained a prisoner of confusion, trapped in a never-ending attempt to gain the love and approval of my father. Neither of these men fully received the paternal love they needed and hence were unable to give of their own hearts as freely as I needed. My beloved Granddaddy Graham had abandoned my dad when he was just a boy, running away with another woman and leaving my Grandmother Cleo with two small children to provide for during the Depression.

When Martin was thirteen, his father dropped dead of a heart attack while tripping on LSD.

When I became pregnant, Martin refused to become a father, having had one son already against his will. He accompanied me to the clinic in the summer of that year and paid for an abortion. Having my insides sucked out by a vacuum cleaner left more than a hole in my womb. It left a hole in my heart. And because we couldn't stay away from each other, a serious infection soon followed. On what would have been my due date, Easter Sunday, I dreamt of giving birth to a little girl who had a congenital defect known as a "hole in the heart." A mirror image of me, she spoke words of gratitude for aborting her because she would have caused me more grief. She told me that I had to learn to love the little girl child inside myself and turn my back on all that was not love.

With my help, the passive solar adobe house Martin had designed and built was finished during our time together. As soon as it was done, Martin told me our three-year relationship was also finished. He drove off in the dusk of a Sandia Mountain sunset.

Anger boiled in my bloodstream. The bitter taste of gall rose up in my chest and curdled in my throat. Licking my wounds, I vowed that the only man I would ever fully give myself to again would be one who could give me the Taj Mahal.

7

Isis ~ Egyptian Serpent Goddess

> Many names had the wondrous Au Set: Mistress of the Cosmos, Ruler of the House of Life, Sovereign of all that is Miraculous, Almighty Lady of Wisdom, Mother From Whom All Life Arose, Primeval Lotus Nefertim, Establisher of Justice, Champion of Righteous Law, Giver of the Gift of Abundance, Inventor of Agriculture, Designer of the First Sail, Planter and Harvester of the First Flax, Inventor of the Loom, Source of the Healing Herbs, Owner of the Throne, Magistra of Fate, The One Who Separated Heaven and Earth, Roadmaker of the Paths through the Stars, Controller of the Wind and Thunder, Restorer of Life, She Who Makes the Universe Spin 'Round. What in heaven or on earth was not of Her making?
>
> —Merlin Stone
> Ancient Mirrors of Womanhood

Fed up with relationships, I threw myself into the rigorous practices of the Sufi Order, reaching profound states of ecstasy through breath and movement. Sexual fire turned into spiritual fire. Now celibate, my corporeal energy burned through dance, yoga, and the chanting movement meditations called Zikhr. I fasted, studied the Koran, and performed Salaat—an Islamic prayer ritual—five times a day facing Mecca. And I became a whirling dervish in the tradition of the Mevlevi Order of Jelalladin Rumi, the mystical poet.

On August 15th, the feast day of Mother Mary's Assumption into heaven, I whirled for several hours in the meditation room overlooking the mountains. A violent lightning and thunderstorm churned outside. The electrical charge in the air was palpable, and as I whirled, a vision sparked within me. Isis, the ancient Egyptian Goddess, Mother of All, appeared. She was resplendent with twin serpents entwined in her crescent moon and sun disc crown, and the golden cobra, *Uraeus*, sprung from her forehead. My legs shook, and I feared that I might lose my balance. But then, from underneath my shoulders, her majestic wings lifted me up into a continuous spinning orb of white light. She merged with my being. My eyes became her eyes. My hands became her hands. My heart was hers. And then she spoke, her words resounding through my body. "You are my priestess, daughter. I have come to claim you back into my lineage. From now, through the rest of your life, you will serve me." She gave me instructions to make a dance in her honor. Why she chose me was a mystery, but I felt impelled to fulfill her wish.

At the end of the whirling meditation, I fell into a sweet, blissful sleep, wrapped in a Mexican blanket and curled in a fetal position on the floor. When I woke, the sky was turning magenta, and the air had been washed clean from the storm. I floated down the muddy road to my campsite. Suddenly, a large snake with a diamond-shaped head crossed my path and poised itself on a flat rock, shaking its cicada-sounding tail as if to say, *"SSSee, I told you sssooo…"* Then it swiftly disappeared into the sagebrush.

I jumped over puddles in the path and shot back up the trail toward my teacher's house. Arriving out of breath, I blurted out my vision of Isis and the snake's subsequent appearance.

His calm response was, "You are from the Pyramids. I see them in your eyes. The snake is an auspicious symbol. You are waking up."

In my tipi that night under the celestial vault of the sky, I dreamt I was in Egypt. The conical tent built around several pine branches meeting to form a smoke hole at the top turned into a spinning pyramid that transported me to Isis's island temple at Philae.

Towering columns were richly painted with turquoise, lapis, and gold. The temple walls, carved with the image of the Goddess and inscribed with hieroglyphics, recounted the story of Isis and her husband, Osiris. Egyptians gathered in droves to praise their queen in elaborate ceremonies. I saw myself as one of many priestesses in a procession, carrying lotus flowers and performing sacred dance rituals in her honor.

When I returned from the mountains, I choreographed the dance to Isis as she had requested and performed it in my first solo concert, *A Woman's Rites*.

~

Dressed in a lapis lazuli beaded gown with a jewel on my third eye and my hair in many braids, I begin the dance in the kneeling pose of Isis. *Mudras*, sacred hand gestures, depict the lotus blossom of the heart opening its petals and offering love. As I rise to my feet, my hips circle and my torso undulates to symbolize the serpents of Isis ascending to the crown to awaken wisdom. In a whirling trance, as the embodiment of Isis, I bestow a blessing to the people.

~

On a kinesthetic level, Isis showed me that within movements of sacred dance there are encodements that can elevate and transform not only the soul of the dancer but also of the audience witnessing the dance. *Isis* was the first of many solos in what became my repertory of *Healing Goddess Dances*. Through Isis, I would be guided to learn the many forms of the Great Mother Goddess, She of Ten-thousand Names. My body, opened to her wisdom, became a vessel to contain and pour out her precious, nourishing gifts. Her fluttering wings beat to the rhythm of my heart and swelled my breast with empathy for others and love for the Goddess within myself. Isis' supernatural presence inside me became a golden compass that pointed to the true North of my spiritual quest.

Le'ema as Isis

8

Snake Energy

> If we dig precious things from the land, we will invite disaster. Near the Day of Purification, there will be cobwebs spun back and forth in the sky. A container of ashes might one day be thrown from the sky, which could burn the land and boil the oceans.
>
> —Translation of the Hopi Prophecies
> Koyaanisqatsi

Isis had awakened me to the transformative power of snake energy and sacred dance. My meditation practices grew even stronger through a profound connection with all of nature. As I watched the thunderheads form in a brilliant turquoise sky, I knew I could go there, too. By putting my root down in the red soil, I soared up through my spinal column and out the crown of my head, blessed by that dear elder in my childhood and rose to my heaven home with Great Spirit and the thunder beings.

The New Mexico monsoons that quench the desert's thirst during the month of August and the wild bolts of electricity that come with them taught me the power of snake energy, a fire in the sky that brings water to the earth. This torrential taste of water encourages the Three Sisters—corn, beans, and squash—to finish their growth season before the harvest. When the rains cease, gentle rainbows appear, sky serpents containing the fire and water that bridge heaven and earth through their full spectrum bodies.

In the Hopi tradition, a snake dance is performed bi-annually in August to pray for these rains. After fasting in isolation, the snake priests leave their village and search for four days in the four cardinal directions for all varieties of snakes, including whip-snakes, bull-snakes, and rattlesnakes. The snakes are then kept in a *kiva*—an underground home accessible only by a ladder—where they are bathed, sung to, and sprinkled with corn meal to prepare for this ancient ceremony. At the main event, the priests carry the snakes in their hands and mouths, communing with the rain gods of the underworld. It is an auspicious sign when billowing, dark clouds participate in the dance by delivering raindrops upon the heads of the people.

In the earth, snake energy is contained in the uranium mined for nuclear weapons. The Indians were the first to protest the destruction inflicted by man's greed. The Hopi elder, Thomas Banyacya Sr., interpreter of the Hopi Prophecies and spokesperson for the Traditionalist Indian movement, pleaded with the US Government:

> We don't want these weapons made up of the uranium you take from our land. If you take the uranium, the lightning won't come and bring the rains. The uranium attracts the lightning. Take it away and the lightning won't come. You have no right to take the lightning from us!

Sadly, my eyes became open to the demolition of this place where I roamed, this place I called home. I learned that more than 1200 uranium mines operated on the Navajo Nation from 1945 to 1988, mining over 13 million tons of uranium ore. When mining companies tore into these sacred mountains, including Mt. Taylor—also known as the Turquoise Mountain—negative forces were released into the atmosphere. A big monster, *Leetso*, meaning "yellow dirt," was let loose. Many thousands of Native people including the Navajos, the Hopis, and the Pueblo Indians of Zuni, Laguna, and Acoma Sky City were poisoned from *Leetso*, dying from lung cancer, asthma, and other complications. Uranium tailings found in the water supply and building materials continue to be linked to a high incidence of birth defects among native populations.

The plunder of these lands and the mining companies' disregard for the Native Americans enraged me. I fumed with indignation, feeling that I, too, had been excavated. It seemed that the people, repeatedly beaten down by the injustices of the weapons industry, could not achieve any lasting victory. After years of struggle, Congress passed the Radiation Compensation Act, but miners and their families never received a penny.

Koyaanisqatsi, a film produced by Francis Ford Copolla, was pivotal in my growing unrest. In the Hopi language, *Koyaanisqatsi* means: 1. crazy life; 2. life out of balance; 3. life disintegrating; 4. life in turmoil; and 5. a way of life that calls for another way of living.

Without a conventional plot, dialogue, or narrative, this movie is a collection of exquisite cinematography with a highly environmental theme. Driven by the compelling score by Philip Glass, the mesmerizing montage contrasts nature with man and technology. We are lulled by the vastness and beauty of earth as we soar above canyons and clouds. Then, abruptly, we fast-forward through freeways and over rows of giant war machines.

In the end, a rocket launches, explodes, and then spins out of control until it burns and crashes to the ground in a dark and foreboding commentary on our present and future.

At the end of the film, I sat alone in the theater, weeping, as hundreds of people filed out. I wept and wept until the usher finally asked me to leave. For days and weeks afterward, nagging questions pervaded my mind. Are we to stand passively by and watch our world be destroyed? Are we to remain mute to these sins against Mother Earth and humanity?

No film had touched me so deeply. All my unexpressed fears were displayed boldly on the big screen. This apocalyptic vision inspired me to produce my first political piece, choreographed to the songs "Major Tom" and "Koyaanisqatsi."

"Major Tom" captured the climate so prevalent at the time of the space program during the 80s. President Ronald Reagan tried to convince the American people that the Strategic Defense Initiative, also known as Star Wars, would save us from a nuclear attack from the Russians. In truth, it was an excuse to exploit nuclear energy to militarize space. Fearing a bad science fiction idea might become reality, many activists worked diligently for the Nuclear Freeze Campaign.

(*Outer Space Audition Piece for the Boys + Mourning Mantra*) x 1 = *Father Sky/Mother Earth* is a composite piece consisting of two dances that when added together make one piece that offers a reflection of the masculine and feminine principles operating on the planet at this time. While the masculine aspect of our modern society is developing the use of nuclear technology and striving to pioneer the final frontier of space, the feminine aspect pleads for reverence to be given to our earth home, Gaia.

Combining gestures of American Sign Language with acrobatic Break Dancing (as learned from my students at the high school where I worked), the first part of the dance took shape. "Major Tom" is about an astronaut who loses contact with ground control after the engines of his spaceship fail. Cast adrift in the universe, he realizes that he is lost and will never return to earth and his family. His moment of enlightenment comes when he accepts that he is coming home to his creator.

To set the scene, a filmmaker friend created a marvelous movie as a backdrop for the dance from stock footage of astronauts and launching rocket ships.

~

As Major Tom, with my long hair tucked under a rainbow headband, I wear a blue flight jump suit and green Converse high-tops. I feel cocky, cross-dressed in my space suit, performing teen boy moves.

As the curtain goes up, I stand with my back to the audience and mime playing an electric guitar. From their perspective, it looks like I am stroking something else. I turn to face them, continuing my rhythmic, jerking movements. This leads to an exciting break dance sequence that includes moves such as the Atomic Drop, Dolphin Dive, Worm, and Moon Walk. Ignorant of my peril, I put on a shit-eating grin until the moment when I realize I'm lost in outer space, drifting away.

~

In part two of the dance, *Mourning Mantra*, I wore a flesh-toned, sleeveless Danskin and a ¾ length skirt with slits that revealed my legs, resembling a ceremonial loincloth worn by ancestors. It conveyed the simplicity and nudity of birth. The dance itself affirms the guiding feminine principle that, if honored by humans, will enable the earth to bloom again and all people to unite in peace for a long time to come.

A symbol known to the Hopis as Mother Earth is a seven-circuit labyrinth, almost identical to the classic Cretan labyrinth of the Minoans. This symbol became the foundation of the choreography. The lines of the form lead around and through the center in the Four Directions. It is a representation of the stages of life: the unborn child within the womb of Mother Earth, emergence from our mother's womb, our journey in this life, and our return to the Earth Mother at our death.

The music from *Koyaanisqatsi*, with its droning chant played by a pipe organ, is a ritual dirge that deserved expression through dance. I called it *Mourning Mantra* because it felt like all four corners of the planet were in mourning for the loss of our connection to her as our Mother.

∼

I lay on the floor in the center of the stage in the fetal position with my back to the audience, slowly moving like an amphibian-like creature, swimming through a primordial sea. Rolling, tossing, turning continues till my being changes into a mammalian creature crawling on all fours. Arriving at the portal, I find my feet and emerge. My palms lift up in praise to the Father Sky and Grandfather Sun as I offer myself to Mother Earth and dedicate my life to her healing.

My hands make the sign for "weep" while my feet trace an infinity symbol on the earth. My tears fall to the ground, symbolic of the rains fertilizing the earth. I drop to my knees and onto my belly and slide through the birth canal until the crowning moment. My head and face pop up as the light fades to black.

∼

The message of these dances stands the test of time and remains a personal favorite in my repertoire; however, it opened to a small audience. Although it helped to convert my frustration into art, I realized that my fierce, political vision lacked the right forum. No one was doing political dance in New Mexico, and I felt misunderstood. It was time to move on.

But to where?

Kathleen in the Mountains of New Mexico

9

Snake Lover

On Valentine's Day 1984 I met a man, Élan, at a dance concert called *Qualities of Love*. The performance took place in Bernalillo, New Mexico, at an old schoolhouse that had been transformed into the Zocalo Theatre. Élan, on the road with his current girlfriend, came to watch his ex-girlfriend perform and ended up meeting his future wife.

During the cast party after the performance, he asked me to dance with him. Black curly hair fell over his shoulders and silvery blue eyes sparkled under thick, dark eyebrows. He slid his hand around my waist and escorted me to the dance floor. Steps in sync, with leans and lifts, we rocked to the pulsating beat of the music.

My body was out there, but my heart stayed guarded. I knew too well the antics of charismatic "lover boys" who would woo to get into my bed, only to disappear the next morning.

At the end of the party, I invited Élan and his girlfriend to stay with me in my apartment in Albuquerque. They took me up on my invitation and stayed several days before leaving for Canada. While I worked as a schoolteacher during the day and danced at night and on weekends, my guests visited the Old Town.

When I told Élan about my "Major Tom" dance, he revealed similar views on the dangers of nuclear technology. In fact, he had been in California working on the Nuclear Freeze Campaign. I told him about what was happening here.

"New Mexico is going to be the first state to glow in the dark!" I told him, clenching my fists and slamming them on the table. "The first atomic bomb was created at Los Alamos Scientific Labs and tested at the Trinity Site on Apache land. This state is full of the raw materials used in nuclear energy, and then they dump nuclear waste here!"

Riled up, we went to a club to see the premiere of the "Major Tom" music video. His girlfriend was tired and decided not to come in with us. She slept outside in their van.

We had a blast dancing to the video. At the end of the song, Élan kissed me unexpectedly. I had thought we were just friends, comrades in the dance. When he asked to sleep with me, I refused. He was with his girlfriend, and it felt wrong to violate another woman's circle. Even so, his kiss lingered like sweet juice on my lips.

Before he left that winter evening, Élan told me about a company in California called the Wallflower Order Dance Collective that he felt would welcome my expressive and sometimes outspoken choreography. In the spring they came to Albuquerque and I saw them perform. An intense spirit resonated through their work. The dances, with themes of political and environmental injustice, incorporated martial arts and American Sign Language. These were the strongest and wildest women I had ever seen on stage.

In the late summer, I traveled to Berkeley where women from all over the world came to participate in a residential training with these Amazons. It was activism through art, and I had found my niche. By fall, I packed my meager possessions in the car and drove across the desert, ready to find my tribe.

Two feminist friends I met at the workshop rented me a room in their house. I walked into this new home and my first ritual that *Samhain* night. On the Celtic calendar, or wheel of life, October 31st is the Pagan New Year. Ceremonies held on this special night of nights, when the veil between the worlds is thinnest, honor our ancestors and the spirit world.

As I entered the candle-lit room, the women sat in a circle on the floor, smudging themselves for purification with burning sage and the smoke of sweetgrass. They cast a circle with salt and invoked a pentacle with their knives. The Four Directions—East, South, West, and North—were called into the circle. We chanted Goddess names, sang songs, and prayed for peace. We ended the ceremony by envisioning our dreams for the future. I wished for true love. Welcomed within the loving embrace of sisterhood, this new place became home.

There was much to learn in those days about gender, race, culture, and counter-culture. The Bay Area was a hotbed for free thinkers. There was permission to be myself that had been sorely lacking in my Texas and New Mexico days. It was in Berkeley that my dance found a voice to express my angst over the destruction of the sacred lands in the Southwest. Dance for social change became the focus of my choreography throughout the eighties.

Though the Wallflower Order Dance Collective eventually disbanded, I continued to be a soloist with occasional roles in companies in the Bay Area. I produced a concert with my friend called *Lightning Strikes*, where we each performed our political and spiritual dances for sold-out audiences.

During this time, I found steady work as a creative movement and preschool teacher in private schools. One bright day in June, while finger painting with the children, I created a picture of two soul mates riding on a magic carpet together. When I returned home, a letter, covered with yellow forwarding address labels and foreign stamps from Canada, was waiting for me. It was from Élan.

When I opened it, a photograph slid out that his girlfriend had taken of me in New Mexico, standing next to a wooden Indian in front of an old adobe building. Although two years had passed, Élan had just now developed the film and discovered the photo. To my delight, he mentioned that he was touring with the Danny Grossman Dance Company and would be in San Francisco that very week. I called immediately. We met that evening at the Blue Nile Ethiopian restaurant where we enjoyed a sensuous meal, eating with our hands and lingering for hours in conversation.

As we stood up to leave, Élan said, "I'd love to spend more time with you. Are you free? Do you have a hot date this weekend?"

"No, but I sure could use one," I crooned.

We jumped into my beat-up green Chevy Impala and sped to my house.

Leading Élan upstairs, I glanced back at him and coyly asked, "Are you willing to please me or are you just after a piece of ass?" There was a longing in my heart to be truly loved by one man, the right man.

Élan paused in the hallway. "Of course I want to please you!"

A few weeks prior to receiving Élan's letter, I had set up an altar with precious objects in pairs: two seashells, two teacups, two stones, and two candles. Also included was a picture of the Taj Mahal, symbolic of the beautiful home I hoped to share with my Beloved. Each night, I lit the candles and invoked a soul mate through my prayers, "God, I want an egalitarian relationship. Send me a man who is my equal NOW!"

I hadn't expected it to happen so soon.

Élan was a good lover, strong yet gentle. Our bodies fit just right. The best part was his open heart. He rubbed his chest into mine and kissed me fervently until all my reserve about whether or not he wanted to please me melted away.

He later mused, "That one night led to the rest of our lives."

Élan spent every night of his tour with me. We lost ourselves to each other in endless hours of conversation, good food, dance, sex, and sleep. On an afternoon stroll by the ocean, we found a private spot and made heavenly love on the beach.

While he held me in a strong embrace and looked into my eyes, Élan whispered, "You've surprised me...all these years, I didn't know who you were. I think you are my soul mate."

Tears slipped from my eyes as I turned my face away. I wanted to believe him. I knew he was the One, but could I allow myself to trust in his sincerity? Not yet.

As we drove to the airport at the end of his stay, I clutched the pink quartz and red jasper stones from my altar. When he got out of the car, I placed them in his palm. "These represent us. Let me know if you truly want me."

A week later, Élan called to say that his current relationship was over. He invited me to come to Toronto for the rest of the summer. A huge sigh of relief left my body as if all that time I had held my breath.

"I will come," I whispered. But inside, it was a shout of joy.

* * *

Sssplutter...sssplatter...sssplutter...sssplatter...sssplutter...ss splatter. Outside the French doors, a lover's song accompanied our lovers duet under the covers. Steady, a beating drum, the rain played a rhythm to match our hearts, synchronizing the two into one. We lay back on the pillows, breathing heavily as the waves of our orgasm subsided. The musky scent of earthworms rose up from the garden—a reminder of the fertility of all life. I nuzzled my face into Élan's armpit, basking in the smell of his pheromones. The water lullaby from heaven serenaded us to sleep. Wrapped in each other's arms, we slumbered all afternoon.

At dusk, Élan woke me and tousled my hair saying, "Now, my voracious honey-pot, shall we seal our mating ritual with some dinner?"

Dressed in our summer whites, we strode hand in hand down Queen Street West, past street vendors selling their wares and musicians busking for tips. Everyone was enjoying the balmy night air after a summer shower. Arriving at Le Select Bistro, we were greeted with a cheery *"Bon Soir"* from the tuxedoed Maitre d' who seated us at a candlelit table for two in the back of the restaurant.

Smells of garlic and wine permeated the air. We ordered a bottle of Beaujolais to complement our meal of Duck a l'orange. Breadbaskets hung from the ceiling above us, suspended from ropes and pulleys. The waiter placed a loaf of freshly baked french bread and a generous scoop of butter in our basket. Élan reached behind him, unhooked the rope from the wall, and lowered the basket down before us. He pulled off a chunk of the bread, dunked it in the butter, and then gallantly guided the morsel to my lips.

By the end of that visit, we knew we wanted to live together. To escape the oncoming Ontario winter, Élan returned with me to California where we feathered a sweet love nest in a tree house perched on a hillside in Marin. For the first time in my life, I understood the meaning of "dancing on air" when we made a perfect lovers' duet. *Suite Kundalini,* depicting the Hindu God and Goddess *Shiva* and *Shakti,* was only the beginning of what would become an enormous body of work danced together. We soon formed a company called Duet with Soul and choreographed several more dances, producing concerts in San Francisco, Berkeley, and Marin. Élan's grace and elegance as a dancer, as well as his strength and endurance, made me fall more deeply in love with him. Although I hadn't asked for a dancer, Goddess had heard my demand for an equal and delivered me a dancing Green Man—the masculine counterpart to Mother Nature and the consort of the Goddess. My lover was poetic, romantic, and a best friend. He understood my vital force, and he matched it.

When spring arrived, we moved back to Toronto. I joined the Portable Theater Company with him as his co-star, The Lady of the Lake, in an environmental theater production about healing the polluted waters of the planet. That summer, we performed throughout the province of Ontario and upstate New York.

Élan had a dance studio, the Synergy Centre, in his large three-story Victorian in downtown Toronto. This became my Taj Mahal. From an organic knowing within, I created *Goddess Empowerment Dancing* and *Reawakening the Sacred Priestess* spirituality classes. Women of all races and cultures came to celebrate the feminine. Together, we explored oracles, drawing on the insight of the Goddess to reveal our personal truths. Then we danced in her honor.

At last, I was able to make a decent income from my creative skills as well as my spiritual calling.

Le'ema as The Lady of The Lake

Le'ema and Élan dancing as Duet With Soul

10

Snake Island

As a child, my mother used to tell me, "Marry someone who loves to dance." I'm not sure if she said that because of her disappointment with my wallflower father or if she truly saw how ecstatic dancing made me.

Élan has not only shared my love of dance, but also my love of love. Ecstasy was as sacred to him as it was to me. Dance has always been a way for us to indulge ourselves in the glory of the ecstatic.

One time, during our courtship, after an invigorating dance class together, we found a special spot in nature where we were able to make wild love among the trees. It was a steamy summer day in Toronto. We took the ferry to Toronto Islands to escape the downtown heat that intensified and radiated off vehicles and buildings. Cars were not permitted on the Island, so it was possible to walk freely without their intrusion.

Sexual encounters in nature do not often happen for ordinary people who walk in the woods. But this doesn't describe me. The passion in this little body has sometimes been described as enough to fuel a nuclear reactor. But the birds and the bees and the frogs and the snakes all seem to go about their business without self-consciousness, so why shouldn't I?

I attribute the puritanical ethics handed down to generations of Americans to be the very reason we make such a display of how sexually liberated we think we are. The whole fashion industry has us sold on what sexy is, as if the clothes make the man or the woman.

Personally, I would prefer fig leaves to bras, thongs, or boxers. Since I never followed the lingerie trends anyway, that afternoon, I left my panties at home. It was too darn hot! I couldn't be bothered to worry about such proprieties.

We decided to go to a nude beach. Our ride on the ferry was crowded with a bunch of sweaty people who were also trying to escape the oven the city had become. We were all crammed together on the deck, waiting to be released from our cage.

Élan stood behind me, nonchalantly rubbing himself on my skirt between my naked cheeks. I could feel his magic wand rise in anticipation. I kept my cool, though the warmth spread between my thighs, swelling my mound of Venus. It was our delicious secret. Everyone else on that ferry could ride the Ferris wheel on Center Island and eat hot dogs. (Hell, they could even use Dijon mustard for all I cared.) We, on the other hand, were bound for adventure.

No one seemed to notice that Élan had slipped his hand under my blue paisley India print shirt and was caressing my nipple between his thumb and forefinger.

"I'm hungry," he whispered in my ear.

My heart raced at the thrill of illicit foreplay. I'd never felt like this with any man before, never allowed myself to play erotically in a public place.

The ferryboat pulled into the dock, and the cranking sounds of the dropping gate snapped me back into the ordinary reality. We jumped off the ferry and jogged to Lake Ontario, where the lapping of the "sweet water seas" along the sandy beach beckoned us to a picnic. Our blanket was barely down when Élan whisked me into his arms. He carried me out into the water and flung me into the cold lake. I surfaced, gasping for breath. With my dripping hair dangling around my face, I crossed my arms and pretended to pout. As he approached, I shoved him so that he lost his balance and fell backwards into the water, making a big splash. Quick as an otter, he dove under the murky green liquid and grabbed my ankles from underneath, submerging me once again.

Laughing, we crawled back to shore to eat our lunch. Élan took out a plump, red strawberry and popped it into his mouth. He inclined his face toward me, gesturing for me to bite into the other half. I obeyed and the strawberry sharing led to ardent wet kisses.

We went wandering and soon found ourselves on Snake Island, the smallest of the chain of the four landmasses that make up Toronto Islands. It was a magical spot, named by the Native Canadians for its serpent shape. There were no amusement parks, no cafes, and no park benches, just trees and wildflowers and weeds and rocks and mud and bushes. There wasn't even a patch of grass to lie upon. We were in a secluded grove of maple and chestnut trees where no one seemed to venture. Surrounded by lush foliage, I imagined I was in a tropical jungle. My senses opened and expanded. Élan's smell was strong and musky; his lips tasted like ripe berries and his tongue, sweet honey. The warmth was around us and between us. Our serpents rose to meet each other, eager to conjoin.

Standing with his legs out in a second position *grand plié*, he lifted me onto him. I wrapped my legs around his waist, clutching a branch of the tree above for support while he thrust himself into me again and again. We were cobras in a mating dance, our tails locked in a tight embrace, our bodies swaying in sinuous undulations. Our pleasure intensified, crescendoed. With sweat dripping down our faces, we smiled into each other's eyes. Hypnotized. We had become one. Rapturous love. Rapturous. Love.

Soon after, Élan proposed to me. Remembering that special day, we vowed to marry on Snake Island. We planned an outdoor ceremony and purchased enough ferry tickets to accommodate our guests. The wedding day arrived, and with it, a torrential rainstorm.

My groom and I would have been willing to slop through the mud ourselves for an outdoor wedding in the rain, but sparing our guests was more important, not to mention graceful.

What some may have viewed as messy and inconvenient turned out to be a blessing in disguise. The dance studio, located on the Northwest side of our 1800s Dutch Victorian house, got a quick makeover. Situated in the chic Queen West area of downtown Toronto, it had gone through many incarnations over the centuries: a junk shop, a grocery store, and now a dance studio turned wedding parlor.

Rugs were rolled up and tucked away. The portable ballet barre was moved to the basement. Chairs were placed along a wall of mirrors. Every possible concession was made to not only create an ambiance of sanctity but to also enable us to squeeze all our guests into this 400 square foot room. We created a simple altar from an old wooden table and placed upon it fresh flowers, candles, a large crystal, and an abalone seashell smudge bowl filled with dried sage leaves. The altar was set in the north side of the room, home of the White Buffalo Calf Woman and the Ancestors on the Medicine Wheel. Beside it, a large door stood ajar, providing a view of the rain and the earthy, wormy scent of fresh air.

On our heads, we wore wreaths made of miniature roses and baby's breath. We even managed the obligatory white lace dress for the bride and white organza shirt with black dress pants for the groom. Although we wore wedding attire, we were both barefoot. The simplicity, the creative chaos, and our friends and family were all we needed. In short, it was a hippy wedding.

Our guests brought potluck dishes for the dinner reception. The entrees were lovingly prepared and must have tasted delicious, for not a bite was left over. A dear friend baked a special homemade *Yin-Yang* wedding cake—half chocolate and half vanilla—to spare us from arguing over the flavor, while pleasing as many palates as possible. We served sparkling apple cider in lieu of champagne since I had been doing recovery work with Adult Children of Alcoholics and needed to feel safe from booze at my wedding.

"The abundant rain showers this couple with many blessings," declared our minister, a Christian of Buddhist persuasion.

At the reception, she told me that in many cultures, rain is symbolized artistically through snakes. The deities that represent fertility and abundance are also depicted as serpents, part-serpent/part-god, or have serpents surrounding them. When it rained, the Buddha was surrounded by these *Nagas*-cobras, which sheltered and protected him. The *Nagas* also surround many fertility goddesses and symbolize the transmutation of negative energies or toxic influences. The *Nagas*, though invisible to most, were felt by all, and it was a day long remembered.

For our honeymoon, we went to Hawaii. My priestess name, Le'ema, found me one morning as I was getting dressed. The sunlight beamed through the window, shining on a Hawaiian dictionary on the desk. It drew me irresistibly. As I lay my hand upon it, it spoke through me: "You need a Hawaiian name. Flip through my pages until you feel the energy."

My index finger came to rest intuitively on a word, "*le'ema*," meaning unicorn. Since childhood, I have loved unicorns. Once, a seer saw an etheric unicorn horn growing out of my third eye. She told me I would come to understand the meaning of it later.

It wasn't until I met a woman who helped people find their unique angelic presence that I understood my acquired name was more than just a Hawaiian loan word. "Le'ema" was a representation of my higher self.

Solara came to Toronto some time after our Hawaii trip. During her guided visualization, we asked for our angelic name. Much to my surprise, the answer was, "I am Le'ema. I am your angelic presence."

I used the name for the first time at a public event in Toronto in 1991, known as the *Opening of the Doorway of the 11:11*. As part of this worldwide celebration of moving into the Angelic fifth dimension, I conducted a ceremony for hundreds of people. Dressed all in white, we danced and prayed in a ritual dedicated to world peace and unity. This was my first public appearance as a priestess.

Snake Island

Élan and Le'ema
Photo by Peter Rhalter

11

Snake Baby

The moment before birth
the cramping so intense
      the impatient urging
           pulsing

Wanting to take the biggest shit I ever had
bearing down hard
      helps the hot searing pain
           of the ripping open of my insides
                seem bearable

Holding my breath
pushing to expel
      this foreign object
           out of my body

I scream and scream
it's coming, it's coming, it's coming
      each time repeating myself
           raising the volume
                to hair-splitting pitch

The cries of someone being tortured
the cries of the portal of birth

> My baby comes bursting out
> behind me
>   a rocket
>   launched into the warm water
>   of the soft shell-shaped tub
>
> He swims
> like Aphrodite's dolphin
>   at home in the sea..........
>
>   —Le'ema

On November 22, 1989, a thick ice lay frozen over the sidewalks. The moonless night made it feel even colder. We were watching news coverage of people tearing down the Berlin Wall with their bare hands when, at midnight, I went into hard labor with severe uterine cramps and bleeding. Élan began timing the length between contractions. They were only minutes apart now and getting stronger, so he called our midwife. Catherine arrived within the hour.

We had swum with dolphins during my pregnancy, and I was inspired by the stories I read of underwater births assisted by dolphins. The evidence that children born in the water are more sensitive and intelligent also impressed me, so we set up our dance studio for a water birth.

On one side of the room was the portable, pearl-white hot tub shaped like a seashell, and on the other side was a blue futon couch, draped with sheets and blankets. In the middle, we created an altar for this special occasion.

Élan brewed coffee for Catherine, while she kept me company as I hobbled about the studio. Every time I sat down, my contractions would stop. Catherine instructed me, "You're a dancer, Kathleen. Get up on your feet." She and Élan took turns dancing with me before the second midwife, Brigitte, was called. The birth was imminent.

Within minutes of immersing myself into Aphrodite's clamshell, I felt the urge to push. Leaning over the side of the tub, I bore down hard and screamed, "It's coming, it's coming, it's coming…" Out popped our baby, still inside the sac, with the umbilical cord wrapped around his neck.

Catherine cried, "He's born in the caul! It's a double water birth. This is so auspicious!"

The two midwives quickly removed the sac, unwrapped the cord, and showed him to me. I had a son, a "little boy blue." Quiet and peaceful, he looked like Baby Krishna, the blue lord of the Hindus. They waited a few minutes to see if he would start breathing on his own. When he didn't, Brigitte bent gently over him and blew a few "kisses of life" into his mouth. Once he started to breathe normally, I held him in my arms in the warm water, ecstatic to have a healthy baby. As Élan cut the cord, we said a prayer. I felt complete.

But the placenta had not come out with the precipitous delivery, and my contractions stopped. I tried to breastfeed the baby, hoping to jumpstart them, but that didn't work. I got out of the tub and walked around the room, but that didn't work, either. We tried herbs and remedies to no avail. No contractions. No placenta. As a last resort, the midwives insisted we call an ambulance to take me to the local hospital, Toronto General. In Canada at that time, midwives were not legally sanctioned to do the procedure required to remove the placenta, so we had no other option. Off we went in an ambulance to the emergency room at five o'clock in the morning. All the while, I was bleeding internally.

By the time we arrived, the staff at the end of their shift was falling asleep, and the ones coming on duty didn't seem fully awake. Complying with hospital rules, my midwives were unable to help me. I was going into a state of shock from blood loss, and yet, the doctors and nurses took their time attending to me. They didn't get an IV into my veins soon enough, and they started to collapse.

I saw myself float up to the ceiling, out of my body. The hospital staff hovered around the gurney, not sure what to do next. Élan and Catherine, plastered against the sterile emergency room wall, started to panic as they watched the drama unfold. I could see their helpless trembling bodies, eyes wide with the fear of losing me. I was flying, and I was dying.

Across the room, my sweet baby slept soundly in the incubator. At the sight of him, I suddenly snapped back into my body and cried out, "Quan Yin, Quan Yin, come save me. Quan Yin, Quan Yin, come to me."

It is said that Quan Yin is the protector of mothers during childbirth, and she comes when she hears the cries of her children. Over and over, I called out for Quan Yin to come to me. Miraculously, she appeared in the form of a Chinese nurse who stood by my bedside.

I grabbed her hand and pleaded with her, "Quan Yin, Quan Yin, don't leave me."

She looked into my frightened blue eyes with her soft brown eyes and calmly stated, "I won't leave you, my child."

I begged her to stroke my forehead, comfort me, and keep me alive for my baby's sake. Somehow I knew that her presence would keep me in my body, so I would be able to raise my child. She kept one hand on my forehead and held my other hand, while locking her eyes on mine. She ran alongside the stretcher as they raced me through the hospital corridors and wheeled me into the Operating Room.

Quan Yin was able to get an IV into a vein in my ankle. She started me on the necessary fluid replacement and began the transfusion. I watched as the plastic bag, filled with blood, began its descent into me. I was given an anesthetic and fell into a dark abyss. The shaman's death.

Some time later that day, I woke up groggy in the recovery room.

"My baby! Where's my baby?" I cried out.

I was relieved to see that Nurse Quan Yin was still with me. She assured me that everything would be fine. But at that moment, all I wanted was my baby. Oh, to press his tiny mouth against my breasts.

She took me to a semi-private room where a robust Jamaican nurse with a vibrant smile brought me my newborn son. Her lilting accent fell upon my ears like a melodic song. She showed me how to properly latch the baby for his first feeding and congratulated me on having my baby at home without drugs or medical intervention. Her presence was a sharp contrast to the sterile, cold environment of the hospital. Her joy empowered and entranced me, and her warmth transported me to a time and place where the feminine is honored and revered for its natural beauty and dignity.

I imagined myself as one of the indigenous Maoiri females in a Gauguin painting. The voluptuous wonder of ripe, full breasts was a surprise transformation of my body. I listened intently as she told me that at first the baby would be receiving colostrum and that my milk would come in a day or so. She said I might experience a type of milk fever as the lactating hormones flooded my system. She gave me instructions on how to hold my baby in different positions for feeding.

Then the doctor came in and scolded me. "Had you come here for labor and delivery, this messy complication wouldn't have occurred."

After going into great detail about the operation, he told me that the placenta had not adhered to my uterus and was already on its way out through the vagina when I arrived.

I wanted to retort, "Had the law allowed my midwives to remove the placenta, I would have had a wonderful birth experience right in my own home!" But the blood loss had weakened me, and I was unable to summon the energy for a fight.

The doctor ended his rant with, "You're lucky to be alive, you know."

I wanted to ask about the placenta—Élan and I had planned a special ceremony to honor it—but I was afraid to hear the answer. Did it get thrown into the incinerator, along with the cut off breasts and torn out uteruses from other women's surgeries?

My recovery took more than six weeks. The extensive blood loss had weakened me, and breastfeeding was a further drain on my body. Fortunately, Élan was helpful with the numerous demands of a newborn as I slowly regained my strength.

Although the winter seemed endless, and I had a long recovery ahead of me, I was warmed by the love in my home. I had a beautiful baby boy and a strong handsome husband.

I was on the precipice of a momentous year, led by the snake's continual presence in my life. Though I didn't know it at the time, it was the Chinese Year of the Earth Snake, and I, the Dragon Lady, had given birth to a snake child. Not long after, my father—also born in the Year of the Earth Snake—resolved to be sober.

Le'ema dancing with Nidaba while pregnant

12

Nidaba ~ Sumerian Serpent Goddess

> She is often symbolized as serpent or woman with a serpent tail...Serpent Goddess of Wisdom, Divine Serpent Lady of Life, Basmu Usum—Holy Cobra, She who made Her way through the reeds of the marshes of Sumer...She created the stylus to press into the dampness of the soft flattened clay, giving one of the most precious gifts, that of taking what is in our mortal minds and preserving for those yet to come, ideas that might once have been forgotten...
>
> —Merlin Stone
> Ancient Mirrors of Womanhood

In the spring of 1989, I attended a Goddess conference in New York produced by Merlin Stone, author of *When God Was a Woman* and *Ancient Mirrors of Womanhood*. Merlin, affectionately known as the "grandmother of the Goddess Movement," led a workshop in writing and publishing. She spoke of a Sumerian serpent Goddess of wisdom as our muse, Nidaba, who is credited with one of the earliest forms of written language. It is said that the Goddess recorded accounts using her serpent tail as a stylus.

Nidaba's story, buried within my cellular memory, now sprang to life, imprinting itself on my psyche. I felt a sudden desire to have a snake to call my own. The current reptile craze hadn't begun yet, and after phoning several pet stores, I soon realized what a rare and special breed snake keepers were. A final call to an old friend informed me that I would have to purchase my pet outside of metropolitan Toronto, because exotic reptiles were not permitted in the city. Élan drove me to the outlying town of Dixie where I met my first snake, a royal python from Africa. My first thought was that she was an incarnation of Nidaba.

Nidaba the snake was an elegant beauty, with an underbelly the color of milk. Mocha spots, shaped like squiggly puzzle pieces, crept up her back. Her diamond-shaped head, resting upon a slender neck, seemed to be made of the richest brown velvet. I often found myself gazing into her sensuous, dark eyes.

When I brought Nidaba home, I hadn't learned yet of my pregnancy with my son. The complete cycle of fertility, as symbolized by the snake, was something my body was yearning to experience. The soul of the serpent was to be my guide.

In the months that my baby was growing inside my belly, I forged a friendship with Nidaba. In return, she taught me the secrets of meditation. Nidaba's breath reverberated through her whole body from the top of her head to the tip of her tail. When she coiled into a tight ball on my lap, I noticed a settling of my energy. As my mind quieted, my breath deepened, and I slipped into a state of serenity.

The first time Nidaba and I danced together was at a Green Party meeting when I was nine months pregnant. I painted the earth on my burgeoning belly and danced as the Earth Goddess Gaia.

Word spread in the community that I was dancing with a snake. When the National Film Board sponsored a Goddess Banquet on the Summer Solstice in 1990, I was invited to perform with Nidaba. I was delighted, eager to express my newfound image as a snake dancer.

A month before the event, we went on a family vacation, leaving our house and pets in the care of a roommate, Sally, who was thrilled to watch Nidaba. Unfortunately, she left the cage open. When Sally returned home that evening, she stepped on Nidaba who was lying on the bedroom floor. She tried to pick up the frightened snake, but Nidaba bit her and quickly slithered into the heating vent.

I was shocked to learn of her disappearance. I had an important performance to do in just one month, and my beautiful snake was gone! How could this woman, whom I had entrusted with my Nidaba, my totem, do this to me?

"Get out of my house!" I screamed.

She backed out without a word.

My anger did not subside with time. Upon the recommendation of a student, I had a session with a medicine woman. She smudged me with sage and cedar smoke and told me that my path was Beauty and that I was to walk *The Beauty Way*. She spoke:

> The world before me is restored in beauty
> The world behind me is restored in beauty
> The world below me is restored in beauty
> The world above me is restored in beauty
> All things around me are restored in beauty…
> It is finished in beauty
> It is finished in beauty…

I felt tremendously guilty having entrusted my sweet snake to someone who proved irresponsible, but the medicine woman assured me that it was not my fault. She urged me to express my anger and disappointment, but I was not yet ready to confront Sally.

She also suggested that I buy a new snake to bring to the Goddess Banquet. I followed her advice and found a domestic corn snake with skin the burnt-orange color of Indian corn. I called him Maiz.

Bare-chested, with my breasts full of mother's milk, Maiz and I danced together at the Goddess Banquet for more than two hundred women. This memorable, uplifting evening ended with me leading the audience in a spiral dance.

After receiving a splendid response, I summoned the courage to face my wrath toward Sally. I was reading *Medicine Cards* by Jamie Sams and David Carson, which spoke of snakes as a symbol of transmutation. When I called Sally, I informed her that she had received an initiation from Nidaba's snakebite. We agreed to meet to clear the negative energy between us.

Sally showed up with a present—a cute, yellow stuffed snake with a long, red felt tongue. Putting my self-righteous anger aside, I told her how saddened and pained I was at the loss of my snake. Throughout it all, I was impressed by her courage and willingness to face the demon goddess I'd become. It softened me, permitting me to open my heart and forgive her.

A week later, on the day my son turned one year old, Nidaba made her entrance after a lengthy absence. I was out for the day when my babysitter spotted my python poised on the molding near the ceiling of the dance studio. Fortunately, she didn't panic or call the cops or the Humane Society. She simply shut the door of the studio. When I returned, she politely inquired, "Did you know that there is a snake in the studio?"

I ran into the room and cried tears of joy at the sight of my long, lost snake friend up on her perch. What a perfect way to celebrate my son's birthday! This was an auspicious sign.

My husband propped a ladder against the wall and calmly retrieved Nidaba. She was so weak that we thought for sure she would die. Finding a veterinarian who knew how to treat snakes was no easy task. By the time we found a place to take her, I expected to hear we must put dear Nidaba to sleep.

We had to drive through a blizzard to a different county to reach the doctor's office. I ran in with my baby boy, dressed in a furry bunny suit, on one arm, and my snake baby coiled inside a sweater in a Kenyan bag on the other. The Indian Sikh doctor, with a turban on his head and a steel bracelet on his right wrist, glanced at the diamond nose ring on my left nostril and my two babes in arms, and smiled knowingly. I instantly knew he could help.

Nidaba received an injection of B-Vitamins. The pupil slits of her glazed eyes sprang open and her limp body jerked to life. The doctor attentively worked on her, demonstrating how to force-feed her until her natural predatory instincts returned.

Reviving a snake was something no one could have ever told me I'd be doing, yet it seemed like the most honorable and natural thing to do if I was going to be a snake keeper. I had to open her dislocatable mandible and push raw hamburger meat down her esophagus into her stomach with my fingers. Several baths in warm water allowed her to re-hydrate. After a particularly long drink, she expelled the dust balls that were lodged inside her throat from her sojourn within the walls of our studio.

Nidaba recovered, and I have now enjoyed a twenty year relationship with this sweet-natured creature. But while I was nursing her back to health, I was haunted by recurring dreams of being left in a pit of enormous human-devouring snakes. Primal fears about snakes rose to the surface of my conscious mind as if they needed release like the dust balls from Nidaba's throat. Perhaps, I might just glean knowledge and wisdom from the nightmarish images imbedded in my subconscious mind.

In my research, I learned that snake dreams of all kinds are common. Images of being bitten by a snake can represent a person's need to face the worries that threaten them. I considered that maybe the fear of caretaking my sick snake, and her potential demise if I should fail, caused these disturbing dreams to surface. It was true that once Nidaba returned to vital health, the images stopped. And with their departure went all remaining fears of any snakes that I had harbored. But there still seemed to be a missing link.

In legends, Goddesses often shape-shifted into serpents. I suddenly realized that my own dreams were about more than just a hostile snakebite; the snakes devoured me whole, taking me into the gut of the Mother Goddess and making me Hers.

Did my primeval dream state portend the journey I was to take in becoming a Snake Priestess?

13

Shamanic Snake

After the adventure with Nidaba, Élan and I joined a group of folks practicing shamanic journeying. The facilitator instructed us to lay on the floor with our eyes covered and listen to the sound of the drum guiding us into the realm of extraordinary reality. She said the animal that appeared to us three times was considered our totem. Each time I journeyed, Snake came to me.

In the very first journey, I slipped through the sidewalk into a snake nest. A big mother snake reared up. "Where have you been?" she asked. "We have a lot of work to do." She slid inside me through my anus up my spine, down my front and out my vagina. She went up my anus again and spiraled into my intestines clearing obstructions. Then snake entered through my vagina and went up into my gallbladder, where she sucked out seven gallstones and spit them out.

She became me and went into a shed phase. When the skin was shed, out came a fresher, bigger snake with bulging red eyes. She/I seemed fierce. She laid eight eggs that hatched into snakes and arranged themselves in a pattern of the Eight Directions, like a Celtic Wheel of Life. The snakes moved out in the Eight Directions and then circled onto me as a skirt. We danced as they spun around my waist. Then each one took me to a different habitat: desert, mountain, plains, jungle, tundra, marsh, forest, suburb, each with a different climate.

After this journey, I felt very churned up inside, and sure enough within twenty-four hours, my body went into a major purge. As a result, I was healed from the inside out. My fear of Snake vanished and I accepted her as my ally.

In another journey, Snake took me through an underground cavern to meet a man and a woman in an alcove for healing and renewal. I was stripped, bathed, and placed on a wheel where I was spun around in the presence of huge crystals until purified and filled with light. Then the man and woman took me to the top of a mountain where a giant anaconda skin was positioned on me, and I was told to dance my light. Light poured out of me in all directions, and people had spontaneous healings. A celebration ensued with everyone joining in a wild trance dance. I went back through the crystal cavern with my snakeskin and the couple. When we emerged, they introduced me to the world.

In yet another journey, I traveled to a spot in New Mexico where I descended into *Kiva* via a ladder to meet Snake. She hissed, "Surrender to your journey, sister," as she grabbed me and constricted me to death. I enjoyed being strangled in all parts of my body. I slid down her throat, being swallowed by her undulating contractions. I saw myself being digested and becoming excrement. She shit me out into my garden, where I became a seed, fertilizing myself. Then I sprouted through the earth as a tiny white crocus.

The synchronicities of snake journeys and daily life soon became evident. By this time, Liam was two and a half years old and ready for preschool. I looked at several places around town, but they all seemed too claustrophobic for my little snake son. Then, as I was flipping through the yellow pages, one school stood out: Waterfront Montessori School on Toronto Islands.

We checked it out the following day, a bright spring morning. From the dock at Lake Ontario, Liam and I boarded the ferryboat and headed over to Ward's Island. This largest landmass in the chain of Toronto Islands is home to a handful of tiny tree houses that look like they come out of a Robinson Crusoe story. The school is located in this charming rural setting, just fifteen minutes from the clamor of the busy downtown scene where we lived. It seemed idyllic for our son.

The teachers greeted us with genuine warmth. They showed Liam around and included him in the opening circle as well as in the daily activities with the other children. Liam loved it all and fit in beautifully. Two of the children, a boy who sported a vest and red bow tie and his younger sister who paraded around in a party dress with lace and ribbons, quickly befriended Liam on the playground during recess.

Our visiting time ended after lunch, so we took our leave. I swooped my toddler up in my arms and walked briskly toward the lake across a grassy field surrounded by giant chestnut trees where I set him down. As we meandered through the green clearing, I noticed some squiggly movements at my son's feet. I stooped over to get a good look in the grass. A baby garter snake with checkered scales and a vivid red stripe down its back stopped moving and remained still as if he was hiding.

I snatched the lithe creature up, curled it between the fingers of my right hand, and showed it to Liam. His eyes grew wide with innocent joy as he looked up at the yellowish-green underbelly of the snake. He giggled when he touched it. When it wiggled free from my light grasp, Liam tried to chase it. He ended up rolling around on the earth pretending to be a snake. I laughed heartily at his antics.

This snake in the wild—a petite goddess in the grass—was all the verification I needed from Mother Nature that Liam would be happy at his first school on the waterfront.

* * *

Meanwhile, I was asked to dance at a fundraiser for Starhawk and Donna Read's *Goddess Remembered* film trilogy at the Royal Ontario Museum. The invitation to bring the snake energy into this bastion of male academia thoroughly excited me. Sneaky as a snake, I strode into the museum that night feeling like a guerilla goddess bringing the fertile seed of the Sacred Feminine back into a dry, intellectual institution.

Since I now had two snakes, a corn snake Maiz, and a python Nidaba, I decided to dance with both of them. Dancing with two snakes was even better than dancing with one. Nidaba peacefully wrapped herself around my waist, but Maiz went wild. He slithered up my body, tangling himself in my hair and settled his head upon my third eye. This immediately sent me into a trance state, and I was transported back in time to an ancient ceremony of the serpent.

My body undulated, rising and falling as though the serpents were inside me. Two cosmic spirals combined within me, and I felt a gateway of transformation open in the auditorium. I couldn't have choreographed something so dramatic if I had tried. The audience gasped. Women wept for joy or dropped into deep meditation. Something very primitive had occurred.

The serpent on my head reminded me of reading about shamans in the Amazonian rain forest who claim to see a giant anaconda residing in the fissures between the right and left hemispheres of the human brain. This new dance made me feel that I embodied mysteries, which shamans worldwide have understood for eons, but scientists are just now discovering. Through the art of snake dancing, I bridge shamanism and science, left brain and right. The twin serpents unite within me as

I dance to reveal the field of unified consciousness that the sages and prophets have been speaking about for a long time.

*   *   *

Snake, you are my sister. You have chosen me in this lifetime to be your voice. I am learning to speak for you. I am learning to use the voice that you do not have.

Limited to a warning hiss or rattle, you are one of the only creatures on earth who do not have a distinctive call or cry. Perhaps this is part of the reason you have been misunderstood in our Western Civilization.

The patriarchal influence of religions has both misrepresented you and misinformed the people of your true nature. In many ancient cultures you were seen as a fertility symbol—your sinuous body, your belly on the earth. It was considered a good sign to have you in the garden. Perhaps in the Garden of Eden, you were not tempting Eve but were passing on a potent wisdom from the Tree of Knowledge. Perhaps it was the knowledge that we are in a body and must trust our instincts if we are to survive and flourish on the Tree of Life. Perhaps it was the light of knowledge that innocence is not bliss and that the darkness of ignorance is what brings downfall to humans on this earth plane.

The impact that lies and disinformation can have on entire civilizations astonishes me. The characterization of the snake as evil is a falsehood that has kept us from true understanding. The serpent has been symbolic of universal truths from time immemorial. In Native American spirituality, for example, Snake teaches us how to be a universal being—one who accepts all aspects of life. It is a lesson of wholeness, of understanding the life, death, and rebirth process. Snake medicine is a fiery energy that can bring about transmutation on the personal level of our lives. When we accept this medicine, we are able to transmute our heavy leaden self into gold like an alchemist.

This is why the symbol of snakes in the Caduceus—two serpents intertwined around Thoth's staff—is still seen on pharmacies today. The Caduceus from ancient Egypt represents healing through the process of alchemy. It is a symbol that modern medicine aspires to live up to, and indeed modern medicine has saved many lives through the use of drugs. But alchemy really refers to an inner invisible process that takes place as a result of the melding of opposites. Just as in the teachings of *Tantra*, alchemy occurs when a complete acceptance and understanding of the male and female principles within each organism creates a merging of the two into one, birthing a divine energy.

Snake, you are my sister. I honor you. You live inside me as my spine, guts, brain, inner ears, and nerves. You are my instinct and my passion. I offer these words as your voice, as a prayer for the transformation of human world.

Snake, you are my sister.

14

Kali Ma ~ Hindu Serpent Goddess

Kali, Hindu Goddess, sprang forth from the brow of the Great Goddess Durga to annihilate demonic male power. Western culture does not have an image of the strong woman whose contact with her primal power and wrathful wisdom is welcomed and actually nurtures us. In this Kali Age we are experiencing a resurgence of the divine feminine spirit in all her aspects. Kali is presented here in Her warrior aspect, dancing in the cremation grounds. "Why is Mother Kali so radiantly black? Because she is so powerful, even mentioning her name destroys delusion. Because she is so beautiful, Lord Shiva, Conqueror of Death, lies blissfully vanquished beneath her red-soled feet."

—Lex Hixon
Visions of the Goddess and Tantric Hymns of Enlightenment

Kali Ma! What a powerful feminine archetype, the Hindu Mother of the Universe—a Triple Goddess of creation, preservation, and destruction. Kali is the ultimate force of change and transformation. One must be careful what one asks for when worshiping her.

When I began my relationship with Kali, I did not consciously understand the immense power I invoked or how much change she would bring into my life. It was on my fortieth birthday that she called to me, requesting to join my repertory of *Healing Goddess Dances*. Earlier in my work, Isis, Aphrodite, and Green Tara had graced me with their presence through Terpsichore, but dark Goddesses—Inanna, the Black Madonna, and Kali—were now asking for expression.

The divine paradox, Kali is a wild mixture of gentle and severe, sublime and ridiculous, light and dark. She is certainly not the West's white-washed-virgin-standing-in-the-clouds version of Divine Mother. As a Goddess of death, she is jet black with a third eye on a hideous face and great tusks. Her tongue hangs out, dripping blood. She wears a cobra around her neck and a garland of skulls. Sometimes she wears a girdle of serpents or bracelets of snakes. Kali is often depicted as a warrioress with four arms. Her two right arms extend, palms open, in a gesture of fearlessness. On her left side, one hand clutches a bloody sword, the other, a severed head. The divergent sides of Kali embrace a universal power that includes both positive and negative aspects.

My first Kali dance was conceived as I entered mid-life, my warrior-woman-self arising. Combining my skills of classical Indian and modern dance, I wanted to create a piece that juxtaposed the sacred and the savage components of this deity. My colleague, Deepti Gupta, helped me choreograph a stylized East Indian Kathak dance set to an exciting world fusion composition by Ravi Shankar. Deepti choreographed *mudras* and postures depicting Kali's fierceness, which she had received from her *guruji*, in India. My Kathak dance teacher, Joanna Das, shared a *mantra* to accompany beautifully mimed movements of a *puja* ceremony to the dark Goddess. I wore a black velvet *choli* top and a bright red silk skirt with matching veil.

~

Holding a bowl of real fire in my hands, I make my entrance onto the stage. I sit in meditation and invoke Kali's presence by chanting: "Om Namo Kali Om," allowing myself to become one with the deity. My hands and feet are painted in blood red. With fast and furious footwork, the dance begins.

Enacting Kali's fierceness imbues me with a sense of purpose and clarity and the ecstasy of divine madness. Fingers flicker like flames circling around my head and body, raising a holy fire. *Mudras* illustrate the power of lightning bolts that dart from her wild eyes. I mime brandishing a sword, chopping off a head, drinking the blood, and then adding it to the garland of skulls of her decapitated lovers around my neck.

Outrageously intoxicated with my kill, I swagger with pride then thrust a trident into a demon and do a final victory dance of the destruction of ignorance. My feet stamp a steady pattern of beats as I spin in swift *Jaipur* turns to a sizzling finale as the lights fade to black.

~

I danced the Kali piece in Toronto before my family headed south to what I humorously dubbed "Kali-fornia" in December 1993. Élan's mother needed help after his father had passed away. Ruth was the ungrateful mother-in-law from hell, to put it mildly. Hardened with old age, she was unable to receive much comfort from us. She was a source of constant criticism, even telling my own mother that she couldn't stand our son. As for me, I was the daughter-in-law she liked least, perhaps because I was the *Shiksa* who stole her baby boy's heart. He was the apple of her eye, and I could never be good enough for him.

I had often thought of myself as the wild Catholic girl who had liberated Élan from the stronghold of his Jewish mother's clutches. But eventually I realized that I was actually the good little Mother Mary-revering Catholic girl who continued to dote on Ruth's youngest son with equal or greater fervor. Being the oldest of four children, I knew well how to care for younger siblings. Over time, I would gain understanding of how the dynamics of our respective birth orders played themselves out in our marriage.

It was only a month after our move when Kali showed up full force. An earthquake of 6.7 on the Richter scale slammed Southern California, causing severe damage to the region. It was as if the wrathful, fanged Kali-Ma had been rattled loose from the bowels of the earth. Fortunately, we were returning from a vacation along the coast and were staying in a small beach town motel 200 miles from the epicenter. Liam, then only four years old, started wailing seconds before it hit. When the shaking and jerking began, we thought that maybe someone had dropped something heavy downstairs or that a couple of drunks were slugging it out. We naively went back to sleep. It wasn't until the next morning that we realized the magnitude of the quake.

We waited a day for the panic to subside before heading back to Los Angeles. Daily aftershocks, sharp as the original quake, kept me in a state of distress. Despite the upheaval, most Californians continued to prefer earthquakes to snow. Not me. All I could think of was returning to Canada and curling up under my goose down comforter. For several nights, I couldn't sleep until four in the morning—the time the earthquake had struck. It was impossible to meditate, much less relax.

Still, it was somewhat amusing to see that within forty-eight hours, peddlers on the streets were selling T-shirts that said, "I survived the Northridge Quake." Another read, "Floods, Fires, Earthquakes, Riots" on the front, and on the back, "Been there, done that, got the T-shirt." Only in "Kali-fornia" could one experience such whimsical phenomena.

In the midst of the chaos, we found a house to rent in the area. A year later, we were burglarized. Most everything was stolen, including my beautiful hand-made belly dance costumes and the classical Indian dancing bells—*gungurus*—that had been blessed by my teacher and that I had worn around my ankles while dancing to Kali. I sensed that all the upheaval was a manifestation of the unsettling aspect of Kali energy coming into my life. Elizabeth U. Harding, in her book, *Kali: The Black Goddess of Dakshineswar*, sums up Kali perfectly when she says:

> Mother Kali creates when she feels like it and then again destroys her creation when she feels like it. All in fun—just like a child who spends a long time to build a sand castle with great care and, then, on the spur of the moment, destroys it with great delight... The devotee who surrenders to the Divine Mother obtains everything. Joy in life and joy in death. All becomes bliss, and all becomes play.

I believe that Kali, as an emanation of Divine Mother, is the shit-eating Goddess. She loves it when we humble ourselves enough to give her our ugliness and the irritations of our puny lives so that she can turn us into pearls. As a dragon Goddess, Kali devours all our dysfunctional dross that hides us from our true self. It's an act of love that she devours our fears and hates, and in doing so, removes the veils that obscure our purity.

In utter frustration, I placed my spiritual focus on Ma Kali and gave her the anger, hatred, and resentment that Ruth conjured up in me. I knew that if I made my shit holy, sooner or later, she would grant me a boon.

Kali had shaken my life up so much that I decided to give her a rest and worship her only through *puja* ceremonies. *Puja* is a devotional, offering ritual performed in honor of the deity being invoked. Candles, incense, flowers, and food are offered to the God or Goddess. These rituals are most often performed by Brahmin priests or *pujaris* but can also be done by laypersons in an informal way in their own homes.

Through the diligent efforts of Usha Harding, a Kali *puja* takes place annually in Laguna Beach, led by priests from the Goddess's Dakshinewsar temple in Calcutta. By attending these and other Kali *pujas*, I learned more ways to worship Divine Mother Kali Ma. Kali even lived within us as Ms. Harding also goes on to explain:

> Kali is the mystical indweller in every human body. When she lies in the Muladhara lotus like a sleeping serpent at the base of the spinal cord, she is called Kundalini. When, through yogic disciplines, she becomes aroused, pierces the Sushumna channel and rises upward, she has different names, depending on the chakra in which she resides. In the heart chakra, she is called Hamsa, and in the chakra between the eyebrows, she is called Bindu. Once she reaches the Sahasrara chakra at the crown of the head, she becomes formless, transcendental consciousness.

With the practice of yoga and sacred sexuality, I welcomed Kali Ma in her form as *Kundalini* to awaken me. Through the inner journey of the body, the greatest temple of all, my search for truth continued. My awareness had deepened in the snake energy that Kali Ma embodies as the serpent uncoiled Herself through my spine. She was, to me, the epitome of the Snake Goddess Supreme.

That spring, I attended a Northern California belly dance festival called *Rakasaah*. It was there that I met an amazing woman named Dhyanis. Tall and lithe with curly auburn hair, she had a countenance and an elegance resembling Sophia Loren. Dhyanis was a world-class dancer, teacher, costumer, and producer of an annual Goddess Show. She immediately invited me to participate in her production in June. Dhyanis and I had a strong connection from the start. I sensed that she would become my good friend and dance teacher.

So I drove back up to Marin that summer to perform a solo *Lamia* and the quartet *Mother Earth/Father Sky*. It was held at the Barn Theatre in the Marin Art and Garden Center. An exciting new venue, *Return of the Goddess: A True Mythology in Dance* had two acts packed with women's dances to the Goddess. The beautifully designed set and lighting created the ambiance of a temple palace in India. This was perfect for my *Lamia* solo, a new piece provocative of a *Nagini*—Vedic Serpent Goddess. It was choreographed to an Indian raga sung by my dear friend, Sabina. I was in a dancer's paradise! When the show was over I had made many new friends and knew there was a place for me in this community of dancing women, dedicated to serving the Divine Feminine.

The comfort I felt in Northern California was in stark contrast to the massive upheaval I had experienced 350 miles south. The earthquake, my difficult relationship with Ruth, and the burglary had destroyed my sense of security. I applied California's new tough criminal law "Three-Strikes-and-You're-Out" to my own situation in Los Angeles and made the difficult decision to move across state with my son. Élan wasn't too happy with this. We decided that for now, he would stay behind taking the time he needed to adjust his mother to an independent life.

My devotion to Kali has helped me see that even my anger is divine—that it's okay to have an emotional body that responds to injustices of every kind. Kali has shown me how to approach the edge of death and come back a deeper person for having touched her blackness. She has taught me that saying "No," and ending what no longer serves me or does not contribute to my truth, health, and well-being, is absolutely appropriate. Kali tells me that it's good to be a force to be reckoned with—to be a powerful woman!

In 1994, in the midst of all the chaos, I wrote an article for *Tantra* magazine titled "Kali's Dance," about my relationship with Kali as a spiritual seeker and dancer. I found it greatly satisfying that this article was later cited in such books as *Encountering Kali: In the Margins, at the Center, in the West* by Rachel Fell McDermott and Jeffrey J. Kripal, and *Offering Flowers, Feeding Skulls: Popular Goddess Worship in West Bengal* by June McDaniel. To be quoted in these scholarly works was an affirmation to me of the seriousness with which I approach Ma Kali. And what a boon!

Sometimes we wander away, or perhaps allow ourselves to be led, from our path. Perhaps it takes a move to readjust our position. In fact, Kali inspired my relocation. She was my liberator, giving me a swift kick across the sunshine state. But Goddess didn't leave me just because I packed up my minivan and drove in a different direction. She had more lessons to teach, and, in typical Kali fashion, they would come the hard way.

15

Coatlique ~ Mayan Serpent Goddess

Coatlicue (pronounced co-at'le-kew), or Serpent Skirt, is mother of the Aztec deities. She gets her name because she wears a skirt made of swinging rattlesnakes. Her beloved daughter, Coyolxauhygul, the Moon Goddess, was decapitated by the Sun God and the grieving Coatlicue placed her daughter's luminous head in the sky.

—Amy Sophia Marashinsky
The Goddess Oracle

SERPENT OF SORROW

Serpent of sorrow
you have struck such discordant tones
inside my soul
that I cannot find harmony within my heart
I heard your rattles and your warning hiss
but I could not avoid your venomous strike
that now has me bent in pain and suffering
humbled, in awe at the power of your precise incision
cutting into me
open heart surgery
my wound is raw and pounding

Serpent of Sorrow
you are the surgeon, your fangs are the scalpel
your venom is the medicine, the potion, the cure
for what ails my aching heart
let it kill the vermin, the enemy—my unconscious, fragmented self
so that my heart may be whole again
and I may live
transmuted by the power of your poison

—Le'ema

Within a year of our move to Northern California, Élan returned to Toronto to participate in a special event for Danny Grossman's Dance Company. While we were apart, I did a reading from *The Goddess Oracle* deck. To my surprise, I drew the Goddess Coatlique.

I flipped the book open to learn more about it: "Coatlique is here to help bring you face-to-face with your grief," it said. "The way to wholeness lies in going through your grief."

"Why did I get this?" I asked aloud.

Élan and I had always had a juicy sex life, but my husband had a roving eye, and on occasion, roving hands. My reaction, typically, was to throw jealous fits of rage and then wallow in bouts of depression. When he didn't return several phone calls over a period of days, I felt uneasy, then suspicious.

A week went by with no word from him. I picked him up at the airport as planned. Before the bags had reached the carousel, I blurted out, "So where were you, in some other woman's bed?"

My suspicions were confirmed. "It was only for pleasure," he said, as if that was an excuse.

The meaning of the Goddess card was clear: His betrayal became my grief. All my emotions spun out of control. When I expressed how angry I felt to my homeopath, she was sympathetic to my cause, encouraging me to see that a powerful shift could come from being in this place. She recommended *Horridus Crotalus,* a remedy prepared from the venom of rattlesnake! It was used to treat weeping moods, rage, despair, and a suicidal disposition. I had taken many different homeopathic remedies before for all kinds of symptoms, but rattlesnake was a new one. I thought of the serpent Goddess Coatlique and wondered how this remedy would work.

Shortly after taking it, a deep underlying grief welled-up within me. Something in my core was shifting. As I witnessed the grief coming—experiencing it, yet not being overwhelmed by it—a gentle awareness of the true self began to emerge. I realized I held a pattern of victimization that many women carry in regard to men and monogamy. My outrage was only the cover to the despair that women have experienced universally. Wendy Doniger O'Flaherty, author of *Women, Androgynes, and Other Mythical Beasts,* writes that in Hindu mythology, this type of suffering—a longing for the departed lover—is called *viraha.* Both Gods and Goddesses suffer from *viraha* in stories worldwide.

I took long walks in the woods, seeking out a power spot to sit in contemplation of this mystery of myself, my man, and the world of women at large who have grieved over a lover. Tears poured out of my body into the receptive earth, streams of salty water winding their way back down to the ocean.

Rumi says, "The wailing of broken hearts is the doorway to God." When I had exhausted myself crying, the phrase "I deserve happiness" rang over and over in my ears. It became my *mantra*. How could I permit another person's behavior, even that of my most trusted friend and lover, to deprive me of genuine happiness?

More than just accepting the grief, I began to make peace with it. I thanked the sadness for the information it offered me about my deeper longings and the disappointments in not having those needs met. It was both a painful and rude awakening to be shaken out of an illusion that I had perceived as reality for thirteen years in relationship with this man.

Projections are powerful stuff! Love is blind! How easy it is to be in love with love, a fantasy of perfection. And it is easier yet to project this falseness onto another person, expecting him or her to fulfill our happiness.

I was being called upon to let go of an outworn belief, growing beyond the captivity of a projection of "Beloved" onto my husband. In truth, my husband was not my Beloved. I was the Beloved, and the Beloved was me. I had to affirm my own divinity by uniting the eternal God and Goddess within myself. Like my ally, the snake, the time had come to organically slough off an encrusted casing and make space to be bigger.

Homeopathy worked its wonders of treating like with like. At a Halloween ritual with Caroline Casey, author of *Making the Gods Work for You*, I had taken a vow. "May my venom be my medicine," blurted out of my mouth before I even knew what I was saying. And here I was, six months later, living that truth. My venom, poison that was making me sick, was my unexpressed grief. And it was indeed my venom that became my medicine. Grief had stuck its fangs into my heart, and I had carried that poison in me for probably lifetimes. I was able to accept how sick I was making myself by holding onto this emotion and letting it flow out of me. Those tears became the balm that soothed a bruised heart. And although my heart was broken, it was broken open. I was learning to love myself more, instead of being in love with love.

I thanked Coatlique for showing me the divinity of grief through the symbol of her swinging skirt of rattlesnakes. I thanked her for being my remedy.

Over the weeks that followed this epiphany, a flowering sense of self-acceptance, responsibility, and a new self-dignity emerged. For now, I knew that the Beloved lived inside me as the blending of my unconscious shadow self with my conscious light self. God and Goddess, positive and negative, light and dark, all resided within me. It was up to me to be the alchemist of my own soul. By mixing and melding opposites, by loving all aspects of myself unconditionally, I could become a wise woman.

*   *   *

Our Lady of Guadalupe is often depicted standing on a serpent with a crescent moon about her head, suggesting her origins as the lunar serpent Goddess. The Virgin of Guadalupe...has her origins as the Mexican (Aztec) Goddess, Tonantzin. Tonantzin was worshipped as a Mother Goddess, the patron of childbirth, and was identified with the moon. She was believed to be a manifestation of the Earth Mother known as Coatlicue, or Serpent Skirt, the mother of all living things.

—Linda Foubister
Goddess in the Grass: Serpentine Mythology and the Great Goddess

Soon, rains opened the door to spring, and it was time once again to work in my garden. The appearance of color in my backyard helped lift my spirits. I went to a gardening store and bought rose bushes. I also brought home a stone statue of the Virgin Guadalupe, standing on the crescent moon. I placed her on my deck, across from the wicker swing where I enjoyed my tea every morning. She had offered me solace after my sister, Linda, had died so many years earlier, and now she was back to offer comfort again.

As I sipped my tea on the porch, listening to Bach's music waft through the open windows, the cup slipped from my grasp and shattered at my feet. When I bent down to pick up the shards, the brown liquid seeped across the wood, painting the image of Guadalupe before me. The moment I recognized her, She lifted from the deck and swirled above me. Lulled into a trance by her graceful dance, I became Guadalupe upon the stage. But to my surprise—and consternation—Élan was there, too, wearing the cloak of Juan Diego. We were dancing a duet for Guadalupe, depicting her story.

When the vision was over, I closed my eyes for a second and took a deep breath. When I opened them, the cup lay in pieces before me, but the tea had dried up. Not even a stain remained on the deck.

I rushed into the house and tore through my books on Guadalupe. Tepeyacac, the site where Guadalupe appeared to Juan Diego, was also the Great Temple of the Earth Goddess Coatlique! The Virgin Guadalupe is the transformation and resurrection of Coatlique.

Immediately, I realized that I must choreograph the dance of my vision with my husband. Trying to follow Guadalupe's message of acceptance and forgiveness, I knew I had to sidestep my own emotions and rise to a higher level of transpersonal love. *Guadalupe: Path of the Broken Heart—Goddess of the Americas* unfolded effortlessly in a sublime dance story to Bach's Air, "Suite 3 in D Major." We spent the jasmine scented spring evenings dancing together while Hale-Bopp, the Great Comet of 1997, made a marvelous passage through the sky. With its magical twin tail presentation, it was brighter than any other comet observed in the past thousand years. We danced the duet at the show called *Goddess and God Remerge* on the Summer Solstice that year.

~

I stand on a raised platform upstage with my back to the audience, displaying the silk veil painted as Guadalupe in the turquoise sky with the dark moon at her feet and gold stars on her green mantle with sun rays blazing behind her. Élan, dressed in white cotton peasant clothes, enters as Juan Diego climbing up to the mountain. He finds a myriad of flowers along the steep hike where normally nothing would grow during winter. The Goddess comes to life before him. I open my mantle and rose blossoms fall around my feet. Seeing Guadalupe, he falls to his knees in adoration.

As he gathers flowers, I release the veil and dance with Élan as a human woman. We spin in an ecstasy of joy. In recognition of each other as divine, we merge in a slow motion communion of wordless love. We hold each other tenderly, our spirits expanding in a timeless embrace. Élan lifts me up, facing the audience while my arms open wide to show the compassionate overflowing love of Guadalupe.

After he gently sets me down, I raise Guadalupe's mantle and swirl it around him. Juan Diego swoons under the sweetness of his vision. As I depart,

Guadalupe's veil flutters into his open arms, symbolic of Juan Diego's tilma emblazoned with her image, the cloak he took to the bishop as proof that Our Lady of Guadalupe was real and that her appearance to him was a miracle.

~

Today the Basilica de Nuestra Senora de Guadalupe stands on this site, Tepeyacac, where Juan Diego first encountered the vision of the Indian Virgin Mary in 1531. It is said that an estimated ten million pilgrims visit the Basilica each year, rivaling the Vatican. Five centuries later, Our Lady of Guadalupe's image on Juan Diego's cloak has not deteriorated.

Whereas Coatlique had symbolized grief, Guadalupe symbolized mercy. The sweetness of her presence in this dance allowed for the love between Élan and myself to rise to the occasion. I now understood that marriage can bring lessons in forgiveness and that gradually, I would come to absolve my husband. Despite the infidelity, the bonds of love remained.

Backstage, he wrapped his arms around me and held me tightly. In a whisper that would not carry beyond my ears, my husband said, "I'm so sorry that I hurt you. You are the love of my life."

Our Lady of Guadalupe Dance

16

Becoming a Snake Priestess

Calling myself a Snake Priestess was not something I simply decided to do one day. It was something that came about as an enormous awakening after many years of being a snake keeper, dancing with snakes, and devoting myself to the Goddess. It came after giving birth to my child and almost bleeding to death. It came after years of friendship with a woman I loved like a sister who challenged me to my core and then took an ax to our friendship, hacking it apart like a dead tree. It came after years of making love to my husband with all my essence and then repairing a broken heart from his affair. It came after a health crisis. I do not take this denomination lightly.

The turning point arrived in 1997. A long-time friend, Myrna, asked me to create a duet for us, depicting a woman initiated by the serpent. In my obsession with making dances to serpent deities, I couldn't refuse. I was to play the primordial serpent while she was the woman ignited by snake consciousness to become the embodiment of Medusa's energy. Myrna was perfect for the part with long red dreadlocks reminiscent of Medusa's hair of writhing snakes.

We began our rehearsals in the early spring, preparing for a performance in the Goddess Show at summer solstice. In spite of several months of hard work, resulting in a stunning duet of powerful and provocative shamanic dance theatre, the Goddess Medusa desired something else. The closer we came to the opening, the more anxious Myrna became. Although I continually reassured her, one week before the show, Myrna was overcome with debilitating stage fright. She could not perform, and the producer, Dhyanis, prevailed upon me to do it as a solo. She insisted that my love of drama and the dark Goddess would give me the courage to go forward, so I re-choreographed the piece.

Myrna came to the performance and seemed to support me. In the program notes, she was credited for conceiving the piece, while I received credits as choreographer and performer. A few days later, she called, insisting that I had not given her proper credit. She screamed obscenities at me and slammed down the phone. Then she moved out of the country, never to be heard from again.

I felt that I had been fair and was shocked by her anger. After all, I was the one who was left in the lurch at the last minute. I was the one who was compassionate and understanding of her paralyzing fear. I was the one who taught her how to handle my snakes, how to bond with their energy, and how to move with them. Myrna never acknowledged my generosity.

Exhausted by weeks of rehearsals and having performed in four other dances in the show, I came down with a severe sore throat. I needed to weep, but my throat hurt too much, forcing me to swallow my tears and all my unspoken words.

As the saying goes, "When one door closes, another opens." When I expressed despair to my friend, Tara, she challenged me to look outside the situation and see the vast universe beyond.

She said, "Rise up in your power, girl. Recognize that you have given this woman lessons not only in yoga and choreography but in "snake medicine" as well. In essence, you have mentored her."

Tara encouraged me to view my work as worthy of charging for my time, energy, and years of expertise. She reminded me of the respect that I received from notable shamans, medicine teachers, and authors in the Goddess Movement. Tara encouraged me to seek ordination in the Temple of Isis and become a legal priestess and minister.

I tucked her advice into my back pocket, not fully realizing what she was saying. I still held the innocent notion that if I did what I loved, recognition and money would follow. I wasn't assigning value to my work.

In the name of spiritual growth, I took a brief respite in my beloved New Mexico, visiting old friends in the Sandia Mountains and then heading north to Santa Fe. On the way, I met a polarity therapist, who generously offered the bodywork my physical self needed. Her skills brought my awareness more acutely into the places that needed healing. Some of the techniques learned on this trip have extended to my personal practice, which I've continued to share in my teaching.

In the bright, early mornings, I practiced Ashtanga Yoga with a renowned teacher; in the afternoons, I studied anatomy; and in the evenings, I read about Anandamayi Ma, the Bliss-Permeated Mother in Linda Johnsen's book, *Daughters of the Goddess: Women Saints of India*. My *Kundalini* opened up powerfully, and I was hot all the time. My bliss was being penetrated, and I attained profound states of meditation beyond my wildest dreams. My body became a conduit of Divine Mother's gift of life: *Shakti Kundalini*.

I spent the last day of vacation at my favorite spa, Ten Thousand Waves, immersing myself in hot tubs, enjoying massage, and eating good food. By the time I returned to California, I was a changed woman; my inner guidance told me that having survived many initiations, I was a Snake Priestess! And the Goddess Isis with her great falcon wings, who fanned the breath of life back into her husband, Osiris, would soon confirm it. She would show me the way to bring this new energy into my life.

Lady Loreon Vigne, founder of the Temple of Isis, called to express admiration of my work. A kind and magical woman, Loreon is the epitome of Bast, the Egyptian cat Goddess of joy and play. She raises ocelots and has a variety of exotic birds at her Isis Oasis sanctuary in Sonoma County. She is also a phenomenal artist of paintings, stained glass, and tile work, among other forms. As fate would have it, she had seen several of my dances at the Goddess Show over the last three years, including my Medusa solo. Now, she wanted to produce a concert of my *Healing Goddess Dances* in her theatre that very summer. This was such an honor. Recognition, at last!

Nearly two decades after Isis first appeared to me in New Mexico, here I was in California, invited to a temple of Isis. It was as if she had opened my ears so that I could hear her call, and I, in turn, had followed her voice to this place where I would serve her faithfully in all her glory and radiance.

Élan and I arrived on a morning in August, allowing us time to wander through the amazing sanctuary with Lady Loreon. We stood in the grass, greeted by the sounds of birds and wild cats. Their callings blended in with the sound of a waterfall cascading over slate rocks and pebbles. Across from the lawn where we were to lay a labyrinth for the evening ritual following the concert, we came upon an enormous, five-hundred-year-old Douglas fir tree. Its two sturdy arms branched out a canopy of green, casting shade on the opposing red barn house where Lady Loreon lived. A set of stairs led up to a purple barn that housed the polished wood stage where we were to dance. Light diffused through the hanging lotus lamps and many stained glass windows of Isis, Osiris, and Horus. Outside the barn theatre was a lodge with rooms named and decorated after the Egyptian Goddesses. Swans and Egyptian geese were swimming in a pond nearby.

That evening, several dancers and musicians, together with Élan and myself, performed a concert to celebrate Lammas, the grain festival of summer's abundance. We had a wonderful audience, and I made enough money to pay myself and the other artists. What a joy! And to my further delight, Loreon wanted to ordain me as a priestess of Hathor, Egyptian Goddess of love, music, and dance, with her mentor, Lady Olivia Robertson.

Lady Olivia Robertson is co-founder of the Fellowship of Isis, an international non-profit organization of men and women dedicated to the Goddess. An enchantress in her nineties, Lady Olivia has dedicated herself to the Divine Feminine. Her book, *The Call of Isis*, describes her work in creating the first Goddess-based organization to become recognized by the World Parliament of Religions. She is truly a heroine in reviving the Goddess Religion in the West, elevating it to the place of honor it deserves.

It was in October 1997, at the annual Convocation of Isis, that I became ordained. Underneath the magnificent Isis Tree, Lady Olivia asked, "Who sponsors this woman to become a priestess?"

Lady Loreon, dressed in a gold robe with an Egyptian collar and a crown upon her silver head, stepped forward. She shook a sistrum—a sacred Egyptian rattle used in celebrations—and declared, "I do. Le'ema has graciously offered her magnificent dances in honor of the Goddess, spreading the joy and wisdom of her knowledge to many. She will bring her gifts as a dancing priestess to our temple."

Olivia asked me, "Which three Goddesses do you serve that shall assist you in your ministry?"

I replied, "Hathor, Lakshmi, and Brigid."

"What offerings do you make to Hathor?"

"I offer my sacred dances to the Goddess," I said.

After she described the story of Lakshmi, who rose from the depths of the ocean of milk, she asked, "What do you offer to Lakshmi?"

"To teach healing wisdom and preservation of our bodies through yoga and to provide nourishment through the abundance and generosity of the sacred feminine."

"What do you offer Brigid?"

"I will publish my life story, poetry, and dances to inspire and uplift those on the path of the Goddess."

With each response, Lady Olivia handed me small tokens, symbolic representations of the Goddesses I had chosen to serve: an ankh for Hathor's dance of eternal life, a goblet of holy water for Lakshmi, and a candle for Brigid's holy flame.

Then she placed a purple scarf painted with gold Isis wings around my neck, smoothing it out with care. She touched one hand upon my heart and the other upon my back saying, "With this stole, I hallow thy heart." She set a crescent moon crown with a jewel over the third eye on my head. "With this crown, I dignify thy head." She supplied me with a staff. "With this staff, I strengthen thy will for good." And then, making the sign of the ankh with both hands, she pronounced, "In the name of Isis, I ordain thee her priestess."

She turned me around. "Now, Le'ema, you may give your first blessing to the world."

I bestowed the congregation with prayers of peace, affirming my vows. With tears of joy, I surrendered myself to the sacred marriage of my spirit. I was on my destiny path at last, following my divine blueprint. I knew now that I truly belonged here on Earth to serve as a priestess. Suddenly, life had much deeper meaning than before.

It seemed all would be well. My husband and I had just moved into a beautiful home, built in the 50s, with a family room that would be my dance studio. Élan's career was prospering, and we were fully on the mend. But life, with its twists and turns, refused simplicity. By January 1998, my body crashed. The rigorous routines I had been following resulted in total burnout. Dance, yoga, housework, gardening, parenting, and driving all over the county eventually took its toll. I had pushed myself beyond my body's capacity to handle such extreme physical demands, becoming more and more fatigued until all I could do was crawl out of bed in the morning, drive our son to school, then come home and return to bed for the rest of the day.

When I went to the doctor, my blood work revealed a low thyroid hormone level. It was a slow recovery process, taking several months for the medication to have an effect. Not only did this provide time for healing but also for a personal journey that would lead me to create a new form of yoga.

The *Kundalini* in my body still needed to move in order to balance the endocrine system, but I was too weak to implement a vigorous practice. Overheating was not an option, so I practiced simple floor poses. This opened the lunar channel of the spine referred to as the *Ida Nadi*. The word *Ida* means "comfort" in Sanskrit. This current has a feminine moon-like nature with a cooling effect, the channel of physical-emotional energy. At this time, I had no idea that *Kundalini* did not have to be experienced as heat in the body. It came as a surprise to feel her energy rising so strongly without the burning sensation.

My body loved this movement and wanted more of it. I began performing these poses every day. One morning, I lit a candle on my altar in front of an image of the saint I'd discovered earlier, Anandamayi Ma. I sat with the "souls" of my feet together, rounding forward with my forehead over my toes. In an instant, I felt the *Kundalini* circulate through my body. The Cobra

Goddess at the base of my spine uncoiled Herself and channeled through me in a powerful closed circuit of energy. Her voice inside me said, "This pose is Ouroboros, the cosmic serpent who swallows its own tail."

Sometimes, the Ouroboros is known as the underground Python, coiled in the earth's womb. The Cobra channeled other serpent poses through my body, naming each one as we went. It seemed as though my altered state lasted an eternity. When I was done, an entire set of yoga had been conveyed to me. Cobra then informed me that I was to codify it, continue practicing it, and teach it. Eventually, I produced a DVD, *Snake Yoga: Sacred Feminine Wisdom,* which extends the work to women everywhere as a home practice.

The ironic gift of illness was a "rite of passage" into this new terrain. The Goddess Herself moved into my body and gave me direct knowledge of her divine juice. She burned within me her fires of transformation. I became the "wounded healer," now ready to be a teacher of feminine wisdom.

In the spring of 1998, I officially began calling myself a Snake Priestess when I hosted my first retreat for women, *Finding the Inner Serpent.* Two years later, Lady Olivia gave me her blessing to start my own Iseum, Isis of the Snakes, under the auspices of the Fellowship of Isis. I dedicated my new home for this purpose.

Isis has truly held me in her angel wings and has granted me the boon of teaching this sacred work. Many years have passed since that ordination day. At the time, I could have never known how much my work would develop from my involvement in the temple. I have led dozens of retreats on becoming a Snake Priestess. I have also ordained several priestesses and two noble priests, including Élan, into the temple. Hathor has guided me in choreographing many dances to the deities; Lakshmi, in creating a new healing yoga form for women; and Brigid, in writing this memoir.

As for the future, I envision a lineage of Snake Priestesses who devote their lives to transformation and renewal, women who wish to work with the *Kundalini*, yoga, dance, sacred sexuality, and *tantric* arts. Goddess willing, I shall continue to establish my core curriculum, training and ordaining those dedicated to this path—a modern day wisdom tradition of the sacred Serpent.

Ananda Mayama

Becoming a Snake Priestess

Le'ema is ordained by Lady Loreon and Lady Olivia 1997

Lady Olivia and Élan 2000

Le'ema and Lady Loreon under the Isis Tree

Snake Priestesses in front of Temple at Isis Oasis

17

Medusa ~ Greek Serpent Goddess

> A female face surrounded by serpent-hair was an ancient, widely-recognized symbol of divine female wisdom and equally of the "wise-blood" that supposedly gave women their divine powers.
>
> —Barbara G. Walker
> The Woman's Encyclopedia of Myths and Secrets

To meet Medusa is to meet the mysteries of menstrual blood. In addition to the Goddess Show, I performed the dance as ritual during a Snake Priestess retreat at Isis Oasis. To help me get ready, my husband painted red diamonds and wavy lines on a black unitard while I wore it. I purchased a black dreadlock wig and a bunch of rubber, squiggly snakes from a costume shop. I wired the snakes into the wig—serpent hair crawling all over my head. Medusa's hairdo is the total fashion statement of the goddess tradition. Then I dabbed war paint on my face. On my belly, I painted the *yoni yantra* in hibiscus red. This is the downward facing triangle symbol of the female principle. And I couldn't resist painting red blood-like droplets running down my thighs.

A frightening image to gaze upon, Medusa became a symbol of fear because it is said that to look directly upon the divine is to encounter a powerful and terrifying reality. I wanted to show the intensely focused, inner energy of a woman in her moon-time. For me, often during my periods, I did not want to focus on the outside world in any way.

When overtaken by a strong process of transformation within the self, the last thing I am interested in is the mundane aspect of ordinary reality. I become so internally focused, that to be distracted or pulled away creates disharmony and conflict within myself. I believe that PMS is caused by having to go away from this exquisite time of inner healing and pretend that nothing is happening and that all is fine, when in fact there is an extraordinary inner change taking place that is not only biological but intensely psychic and spiritual as well.

~

I begin the Medusa dance in a coiled position on my side. One of my snakes is inside my costume, along the side of my ribcage, snuggled tight inside the cotton spandex unitard. My other snake is wrapped around my neck. As I open my body along the floor, my back toward the audience, no one can see what I look like or that I have snakes on my body. In almost imperceptible micro movements, I undulate my spine, feeling the waveform of serpent energy deep inside. Silently, I invoke the electrical energies of serpent power to be with me. My focus is in my center, below my navel. I visualize a red-orange glow that fills me and spreads radiant warmth throughout my body. Sliding slowly around the stage on my belly, I stretch up into cobra pose, facing the women. This is the first they see my wild face. I flick my tongue out quickly in the manner of my forked-tongued friends and let out a

"SSS." My mood is somber and dares the viewers to enter my den and witness the mysterious ritual about to take place. Medusa comes in strong now. Her intensity takes me over. I open my body to be a vessel for her strong medicine.

It is said that "Medusa" has the same root as "medicine" and "measure," derived from a Greek word meaning "to protect, to rule over." I feel the wrathful aspect of her energy both protecting me and ruling over me. Medusa requires that every breath I take be a full embodiment of her. I am at once frightened and exhilarated. Time seems to stop. I go into back bend and the dance unfolds. With my legs tightly together, I undulate up to my feet. I rise up onto my toes and pull the snake out of my costume in one prolonged move. Then I turn to face the audience and commune with my snake. Her face is close to mine, and she licks me with her tiny two-pronged tongue. She whispers the sacred secrets into my ear, and as I listen, my excitement mounts. Pulses accelerate. Sparks sizzle inside my body's fluids—water conducting electricity.

I take my other snake from around my neck and hold one in each hand. I squat in birthing prayer pose and send a cord of ruby red light down into the earth from my perineum—the soft tissue between the anus and the vagina—the root chakra for women. As my root chakra connects with the fiery molten mass at the center of the earth, I pull the heat up into my belly and my *Kundalini* rises. The didjerido music keeps my focus deep in the earth. I wrap the two snakes into the black dreadlocks on my head. They make a nest in the snake-like coils of the wig.

I turn my back to the group as I begin to peel off the snakeskin unitard. I slip one shoulder and arm out and then the other. With great deliberation, I roll the skintight costume down my torso, over my hips, past my thighs and calves, and step out of my skin. The audience gasps when I stand naked before them. The flute music flutters, a quickening.

With my hands in a yoni yantra, triangle mudra, I demonstrate the *Kundalini* moving up the chakras, suggestive of the rope ladders to heaven that shamans see in their visions. I pull the energy up from my yoni to my belly, circling the hands in a chain-like movement up and up and up. From the belly to the heart, from the heart to the throat, from the throat to the third eye, the energy moves up through crown chakra, exploding open. The *Kundalini* now floods my whole body. I shimmy, flicker, and quake with the involuntary shaking known as *kriyas*. The sparks fly off my body in every direction.

I fix my gaze, Medusa's look of power that can turn men to stone, on the audience. My tongue comes writhing and hissing out of mouth. I squat in the birthing prayer pose again, this time facing front, permitting the audience to witness the sacred opening from whence flows the blood of life, birth, and the blood of death, menstruation. I molt before their eyes, at once vulnerable and powerful.

You can look, but beware! Do not come near, and do not touch, is the message Medusa sends. She radiates a mighty energy that something profound is happening here—personal and yet universal. Like a snake, I've shed my skin. A quiet and noble enactment of the mystery of life and death has taken place. I am as awestruck as my witnesses tell me they are.

∼

During this ceremonial dance at a retreat, the moon-blood Goddess Herself graced me with my period. I was both horrified and delighted at the appearance of my monthly blood. Since I was now initiating Snake Priestesses, it felt appropriate to allow my menstrual blood to run down my legs. The initiates' faces were wet with tears. I felt like I was standing on the edge of an abyss, and I chose to jump. *Should I walk my talk?* I thought to myself. *Am I practicing what I'm preaching?* I risked absolute humiliation to stay in my truth.

The truth was in the telling, for within a few short hours after witnessing the re-enacted blood rite of Medusa, several women in the workshop started their periods. Some of them had been late. One woman who hadn't had a period in months was overjoyed because she thought she had entered menopause without a chance to say goodbye to her moon-time and hello to holding her wise blood within.

We created our own modern menstrual hut. The sacred objects of Kotex and tampons were passed out with delight and humor to the unprepared supplicants.

A precious bonding took place among us in a spirit of great joy. The Hoop of the Sacred Sisterhood was being mended. Something extremely significant had taken place, and we each knew that the world was the better for it.

Le'ema as Medusa

18

Snake Medicine

Green Leaf
Little vine snake
So small and precious
Like emeralds
Your scales sparkle
With a luminosity
An other-worldly luster
A verdant, scintillating flash
Now I see you
Now I don't
Come fertilize my imagination
The rain forest in my mind
Come curving, slithering, sliding onto the page
Opening like a jungle
Into the Amazon

—Le'ema

I had always wanted a green snake, but since most of them are found in the tropics and I live in North America, I gave up on the idea. One day, Liam made a colored pencil drawing of a green snake stretched across a garden of multi-colored tulips. He seemed to pull the image right out of my mind, a junior Houdini releasing some primordial creature from the trap of my brain. A clown extraordinaire, Liam often entertains me, keeping my mood light and buoyant when melancholy moments creep up.

His artwork was prescient of finding a little green vine snake in the pet store. I asked Liam what we should call the snake and he replied, "Green Leaf. His name is Green Leaf."

Green Leaf was pencil thin and about eight inches long. He didn't have fangs, and his mouth was shaped like a child's innocent grin. We fed crickets to Green Leaf, which he fondly gobbled up in the same way frogs' tongues spring out of their mouths to catch a fly.

We took Green Leaf to Liam's second grade class along with two other snakes, my ball pythons, Nidaba and Monty, and our three Indonesian Fire Belly frogs. The children were thrilled to be holding snakes. They watched as I fed the frogs and Green Leaf some crickets. Like the chatter of birds in a forest, the children's squeaking voices were a delightful approval of me as the "Cool Mom."

As I pulled Green Leaf out of the cage to pass around, I noticed a sore on his body. The teacher noticed, too, and seemed nervous about allowing the children to touch the snake. I quickly put Green Leaf back into his cage, hoping that I could heal him.

"After all, I'm a healer. I've already brought my python Nidaba back to life once." I said to myself. "It's just a little sore. It's nothing. I'll fix him."

Green Leaf didn't last but a couple more days. He died during the night with a cricket lodged in his jaws, his body stiffened like an eerie science experiment. I was upset, but not enough to deny a morbid fascination. I wanted to be the urban shaman who collects road kill animals and uses their bones as sacred objects. Green Leaf's skeleton would make a great snake bone necklace for me, "Snake Woman."

One of my women friends in Canada mentioned that she had used the microwave on some of her road kill so I thought I'd try it. Pleased with the idea, I proudly popped Green Leaf into the microwave on a paper towel and pressed the start button. Within seconds, the entire house was saturated with the stench of rotting flesh. I couldn't believe one little snake could stink so much. I had to cover my nose and mouth with a towel to pull the nuked critter out and throw it into the outside garbage bin. It took a whole day and several sticks of incense to remove the foul odor.

Who did I think I was? Certainly no real shamaness would have behaved so foolishly. I felt especially stupid after another friend told me the right way to get to the bones.

My shaman friend and fellow snake keeper, Lion, illuminated the process of gleaning the bones from the flesh of dead animals. Lion had a natural understanding of these things. After telling him my absurd, "I Microwaved my Snake," story, we shared a good laugh together.

Then Lion proceeded, "If you ever want to do that again, just place the creature somewhere on the earth, away from your house. Put a fine mesh screen over it, and secure it to the ground. The flesh will decompose, and the ants and other bugs will pick the bones clean. It helps to put it in the sun. The screen will protect it from being eaten by scavengers, and soon you will have your bones."

Simple, common sense, I thought. *I guess I didn't really deserve that snake bone necklace after all.* So Green Leaf ended up somewhere in a garbage dump, my treasure gone forever. It would have been a simple ending to my story, but I was to learn a deeper lesson in snake wisdom.

As though Mother Nature was getting even with me for disturbing the dead, the next evening I became ill with a strange sickness I could only have gotten by handling a diseased snake. While sitting in a movie theater with my husband and son, I felt overwhelmingly hot, dizzy, and slightly nauseous. At first, I thought, *it must be something I ate*, and then, *No, I'm having a hot flash*.

The feeling progressed to the point that I had to leave the theater. Panic set in. A sense that I was going to die overwhelmed me.

My husband rushed me home. I was so distraught that I couldn't be touched and could only lay on the bed in a darkened room with a cool washcloth over my head. When my husband or son entered the room, I freaked out as though some large predator was stalking me. My whole awareness was amplified, and I sensed the infrared energy coming off their bodies. I felt a pulsing, red glow around the auras of my son and husband. They didn't need to touch me or make a sound for me to feel their presence. Élan was worried that I was sick enough to be hospitalized. He kept checking in on me, but all I wanted was to be left alone.

I remained in this state for nearly three hours. Had I contracted some fatal disease that was taking swift action on my nervous system like the deadly neurotoxins of venomous snakes? The reptilian brain took me over completely. It was an experience of feeling the deepest primal fear of annihilation I ever had. I became a cold-blooded snake, slow, dull, and sluggish, and yet hyper-alert of my surroundings. Was this the shaman's death?

Finally, sleep crept over me, and when I awoke, it was as from an initiation into another realm. My symptoms had vanished, but the imprint that the dis-ease had left on my psyche would never be forgotten. The only explanation I could find was that I had undergone a "rite of passage" in which my body was shape-shifted on a cellular level into the snake.

Snakes do not have good eyes and lack ears. They are, however, sensitive to movement, light, and shadow. They are alerted to live food or danger in their immediate vicinity through these perceptions. Though I do not have a fully conscious understanding of how a snake really feels, that night I got a sense of perceiving through infrared energy.

Weird, weird, weird, I thought. *What a woman of wyrrd, the natural path of healing, would undergo to gain a glimmer of understanding.*

19

Shopping Mall Snakes

My snakes were hungry, and the time had come to get them food. The school day was over, which meant that Liam had to come along for the ride.

"Don't forget I aced my report card, and I got a Math Wizard button!" he told me with a capricious grin. "After the pet store, can I get a toy at the mall, Mom?"

"Sure," I said.

At the mall, Liam pointed to a young woman's dress shop called Bebe. "Look, Mom, snakes, snakes, everywhere!"

To my surprise, the mannequins in the window wore what appeared to be real snakeskin pants, snakeskin jackets, snakeskin mini-dresses, and snakeskin mini-skirts. Could it be the snake was making a comeback in the fashion industry? Macy's also had velveteen, snake-patterned clothes, and just this past week, a priestess sister had brought me a magazine clipping from *Vogue*, advertising snakeskin Gucci dresses at Saks Fifth Avenue of all places.

Admittedly, I enjoyed a few sensuous snaky outfits in my own wardrobe. Curious, I led Liam by the hand into the store.

I ran my fingers over a slinky mini-dress on a rack. The hide felt like it was made from a reptile. After a few seconds, I determined it wasn't snake. Could it possibly be made from the skins of certain big lizards in the Indonesian rain forest, which I'd heard were now endangered, thanks to boots, belts, hatbands, purses, and clothing?

With my protective instinct aroused, I searched the store for a salesperson. "What are these outfits made from?" I asked the bleached-blonde girl behind the counter.

"Um, I think it's cow hide, embossed with a snakeskin pattern." She batted her blue eyes, as if flirting would make a believer out of me.

I smiled and continued to browse through the store. In front of the mirror, I held up an array of skirts and dresses to my body. They were tiny. In fact, there wasn't a single item in the store over a size 8. I remembered a time when size 8 seemed to be the smallest size for a woman, but here, in this retail candy shop, it was the largest! The racks were loaded with sizes 1s, 2s, 3s, and 4s—formerly a young girl's size 10 or 12. Yes, we're talking age as well.

I decided that it wasn't worth the effort to take off my clothes in order to squeeze myself into one of these cute, trendy, sexy things. Could it be that I was getting old, or worse, old-fashioned? I tried to laugh at myself for being offended by this garb, but I couldn't do it. I wouldn't want a preteen of my own to wear this stuff. After all, what had happened to childhood? Why was our culture so willing to turn our little girls into sex objects before they even hit puberty?

I shoved a mini-dress back on the rack. It slipped off the hanger and crumpled into a pathetic ball on the floor. My slight annoyance grew into indignation. Was the fashion industry, mostly run by misogynist jackals, trying to tell women that we must have a young girl's figure, or perhaps be anorexic, to fit into our culture's ideal of beauty?

I had to leave this shop before I launched into a politically correct tirade with the salesgirl, or worse, attempted to strangle some sense into her.

In a venomous stew, I led Liam across the mall to the pet store with razor-quick "S" shaped movements, similar to those of a desert sidewinder. He was too busy watching a boy glide past on rollerblades to notice my foul mood.

While Bebe had been empty except for the salesgirl and myself, there was a line at the pet store. Waiting in lines are always opportunities for me to turn inward and still my body and mind from the hectic nature of running errands.

At least I'd returned to the real world of grandmas and housewives, I told myself. Nonetheless, I was decidedly different than the other women in the store. I held my silver snake pendant next to my heart and inhaled deeply through my nostrils, exhaling through my mouth on a long, slow, "Ssssssssssssssssss." My anger ebbed a bit, but as the salesperson kept talking on the phone, I recoiled from an impulsive urge to strike out at her. Continuing my "Snake Breath," which I teach to all my students and aspiring priestesses, I finally managed to release the constricted feelings.

As Liam counted the shiny goldfish in a tank, I whispered a prayer of gratitude. "May the relaxed breathing pattern of the snake in repose bring me back to my center." I was grateful that the snake, poised to strike out to catch its prey, or for self-protection, was my guide. "Snake, teach me to protect myself, my family, and my community by striking out at injustice with swift, righteous action."

As I glanced back at Bebe, a sly smile spread across my face like the 'inner smile' of the Buddha. With it came a knowing of the deeper meanings of life through the symbol of the serpent, albeit in the form of young women's designer-wear permeating mainstream culture. Perhaps some of the instinctual serpent wisdom so needed would rub off on society as we shifted into the "New Millennium."

While waiting, a lady in a floppy, red hat told me about some of her pets—an angora bunny rabbit, a cockatiel, and a chinchilla—when our conversation was interrupted by a blue-haired woman with stout, sausage-shaped legs encased in pantyhose three shades too dark.

"Why are you buying those mice?" she demanded.

"Food," I replied, "for my pet snakes."

She glared at me through thick-lensed, pink spectacles. "Snakes!" she erupted. "You have snakes in your house?"

With a tinge of amusement, I started to explain some of the reasons why snakes make great pets, but she wouldn't listen.

Mrs. Busybody looked at my son. "I bet you risk his life by keeping those disgusting, poisonous animals around!"

The lady in the red hat came to my defense. "They sell snakes here, you know. Right over there by the puppies."

Mrs. Busybody lifted her handbag as if she was about to smack the lady in the red hat. I gently nudged Liam back and stepped between them. Luckily, a handsome, long-haired salesman came to our rescue.

"What can I do for you, Ma'am?" he asked.

Mrs. Busybody's resolve melted as the salesman diverted her attention. "Kitty litter," she huffed. "But this crazy woman here is buying innocent mice to feed to her snakes!"

I resisted the temptation to let her know that poor little mice were also cat food. Unlike snakes, who kill with a single well-aimed strike and compassionate constriction before the unsuspecting rodent even knows what hit him, cats batter mice around like a play toy until they die, then perhaps feast on the catch, abandoning the heart, liver, or intestines in a trail of evidence of their playful crime. Or that sometimes cats kill mice merely for the thrill of the hunt, leaving them dead at the threshold as a proud trophy to present to their owners.

"Cat litter is on aisle three," the salesperson said quickly. With a chivalrous demeanor, he led her away from the line of fire.

The saleswoman, who was now ringing up my purchases, breathed a sigh of relief. "Whew! I was beginning to feel like I was being attacked by one of those Right to Lifers ready to bomb an abortion clinic."

At the end of the aisle, Mrs. Busybody couldn't resist looking over her shoulder to give an indignant snort. With her schnoz pointed straight up in the air, she strode off.

"God loves all his creatures," the lady in the red hat called after her. "So should you!"

I slipped the clerk an extra five-dollar bill to cover the lady in the red hat's plastic hermit crab cave. Then I took Liam's hand once again and left the store.

Outside, I leaned down to Liam's level. "Wasn't I supposed to buy you something?"

His face lit up, pleased that I had remembered.

At Toys R Us, my son immersed himself in a seductive array of *Star Wars* paraphernalia. Acutely aware of the American mainstream's cultural indoctrination of our little boys into mindless droids of war, I wondered how to cope with this overwhelming dilemma. Helen Caldicott calls this obsession with war, "testosterone poisoning."

Fortunately, Liam decided against the uglier-than-sin action figures, the droid destroying Lego sets, and the bomb-happy *Game Boy* games and settled for some subliminally satisfying squirt guns.

Happy with our purchases, we headed home.

Family Photo – Fall 1998

20

Cleopatra's Snake Wisdom

Cobra venom may have been employed in initiatory rites and may also have been used by the pharaohs to perform their transition into the afterlife.

—DeTraci Regula
Sacred Scarabs For Divination and Personal Power

One of the last of the Goddess-queens of Egypt, Cleopatra followed the precedent of Egyptian rulers in general and turned herself into a divinity. At an Alexandrian festival she "assumed the robe of Isis and was addressed as the New Isis."

Though she was not a native Egyptian, but one of the Macedonian family of Ptolemies, Cleopatra exercised the ancient prerogatives of Egyptian queens. Julius Caesar became her lover because it was the only way he could annex Egypt to the Roman provinces. By time-honored law, no man could exercise political power in Egypt unless he loved its queen.

...It may be that men who lay with the queen (and therefore with the Goddess herself) were believed to gain immortality thereby, for any man who coupled with a Goddess would become a God.

> Sacred marriage, followed by death and deification, formed the basic pattern of many ancient Mysteries.
>
> —Barbara G. Walker
> The Woman's Encyclopedia of Myths and Secrets

It was said that Cleopatra turned herself into a divinity assuming the robe of Isis. I was ten when Elizabeth Taylor portrayed the legendary Cleopatra on the big screen. The glory and grandeur of the last Goddess Queen of Egypt, one of the greatest lovers to ever live, captured my imagination and stirred the feminine mystique within. As a teen, I imitated her style, dressing in royal purple and gold and painting my eyes with black kohl. I was intrigued with her intelligence, creativity, and passion, but especially, her role as the daughter of Isis. It was years later that I realized my own tragic, romantic complex seemed bound up in Cleopatra's story. Perhaps my fascination was even a sign that one day I would become a priestess of Isis.

Thirty-six years later and just two years after my ordination into the Temple of Isis, the Goddess's image visited mainstream America again via ABCs two-night epic remake of Cleopatra's story. I should have been happy. Perhaps more women would wake up to their queenly-goddess selves. And yet something inside my guts tugged at me, a fear that when the Goddess does emerge strong, beautiful, and powerful she will again be conquered by an oppressive male-dominated society.

When I watched the television starlet slap a digitally imposed snake to her breast, I laughed at this ludicrous portrayal of a legend. No one will ever know the truth about how this great queen died. Some modern investigators speculate that Octavius murdered her. Some believe it was suicide by an asp or a cobra. I prefer to believe that the last pharaoh of Egypt died by her own hand. Perhaps Cleopatra's suicide by a serpent suggests that she was sacrificed for the land. Egyptians believed that death by snake bite secured immortality. When faced with having her soul contaminated by the corrupt Octavius, the loss of her lover, Marc Antony, and the fall of her homeland, the daughter and representative of the Goddess Isis chose to go to the afterlife.

"You have won, Cleopatra." Octavius spoke these last words to Cleopatra as she lay in her tomb. Unfortunately, the Goddess did not win. Rome had conquered Egypt and burned the library in Alexandria where much of the world's knowledge was stored.

The romantic and courageous nature of Cleopatra's death by a poison that transmutes has always moved me. The highest code of honor that a priestess can follow is the path of love. She took her life for the love of her husband, Mark Anthony, and the love of her country. The Goddess was going underground but could not die. She would live forever in the hearts of her people through the worship of Isis.

The cobra in ancient Egypt represented immortality. In modern culture, however, it often symbolizes temptation and sin because of its role as the betraying villain in the biblical story of Adam and Eve. As the Queen of Egypt perishes in the final scene of Cleopatra, she tosses her head back as if in sexual ecstasy.

Soon after the television special, I received several e-mails and phone calls from people wishing to worship the Goddess. One man, who claimed to be an investment banker with a black belt, asked, "How can I worship the Goddess? Would you take a donation?" He offered to tithe to my Isis of the Snakes Iseum. I thought he was sincere after consulting with him several more times.

But when he inquired, "Did you enjoy watching Cleopatra on TV? The death scene turned me on," I hung up the phone. But he called again, leaving a message on my machine.

"Did you receive what I sent?" His heavy breathing was followed by the abrupt dial tone. With a shaky hand, I quickly punched the erase button. Then I immediately deleted my phone number from my website.

A piercing pain in my solar plexus grew increasingly worse. What he had sent me was not a check for the consultation but a psychic hook into my feminine power. I felt his sorcery, greed, and lustful desire for domination. This man was so desperate for female sexual energy he tried to steal it from me. He was a warrior—another Octavius. He wanted the prize of a living goddess to own like a trophy, invading my psychic space like a conqueror in the same way the Romans subjugated Egypt.

The pain lasted for nearly a week until I sought out two medicine women who validated the possession. They helped to clear the energy of this psychic vampire and gave me a lesson in opossum medicine, reminding me that the greatest form of protection against a predator is to play dead. I ignored his calls. Without an audience, his performance fell flat.

True female strength is as awesome as the Goddess Herself. Powerful, beautiful, representatives of the Goddess are both enchanting and threatening to our society, even today and even to other women. Women like me have been in hiding for so long that it hurts almost as much to hold back as it does to come out and risk being annihilated. If beauty and female power are enough to attract cyber-vampires, is it worth being seen? Is it worth writing a book? Is my work with the Goddess in vain?

I wanted to fight back, but sometimes, the only way to win is to disappear, to die, like Cleopatra did. Maybe this is why I have been suicidal much of this lifetime, and why so many of my sisters feel the same. Cleopatra was a living lineage of the Goddess. Struck by the snake, the venom hastened her way home to the clear light of consciousness, to the eternal Mother, Isis. True lovers never fear death for they know death is the road home. And Love is stronger than Death!

One morning, while making love with my husband, all my chakras spun open. The top of my head opened its doorway to heaven, and my spirit flew far away from this dimension.

"If it is God's will in this lifetime, may I never return to the wheel of life," I prayed. "Let our practice of *tantric* sexuality be a rehearsal for my deathbed."

In my lover's bed, deeply merged in union, I am learning to be free—to outgrow the need for a body stuck in duality. I want to accomplish my mission this journey and rest for another millennia in this sweet ambrosia. I do not wish to return in the body for my Goddess. I long to shed the skin of flesh and bones—to be set free to ride the star waves of liquid light—leaving my earthly burdens behind. Oh Death, be swift and sure—like the sting of the snake. And may my heart be as light as Ma'at's feather, that I may be embraced in her wings eternally.

I pray that in the moment of death, I will remember this desire. The Sufi's say: "Make the desire of the mind, the desire of the heart." My heart's desire is that one day, I will whirl out of this lifetime like a dervish spinning from cosmos and chaos into coherence, and that my Lord will come to meet me in the garden, His face shining, welcoming me home. Back to the body of Nut I will return, like Queen Cleopatra.

My trials with the psychic stalker were only temporary, a blip in the universe. What will last is any contribution to the Goddess that I make on this planet. My body is the vehicle to get me there, but it is not needed to carry a message into the future.

In her poem, "These Red Nights" Rose Flint asks:

> ...How can we not leap into the emptiness that enthralls the world? How can we not die beside this path of broken Beauty? This is how. Remember what we do those of us who love the Goddess: we love. Our hearts are stars; still, in the

unseen place without even sight of our healing, we love. We become Nut, our heart-stars linked, holding the Goddess, so we are the arc and the night and the light and the dawn, we are the world's hope and the earth's holding.

Cleopatra's Snake Wisdom

Le'ema dancing in the ancient ways
Photos by Theresa Jasinski; Photocomposition by Eric Bobrow

# 21

Wadjet ~ Egyptian Serpent Goddess

> The cobra Wadjet protected Horus after his birth in the papyrus swamps. She bears a snake's head upon a woman's body. She rules the Eye of Horus that conferred its wearer physical strength and protection. She initiated the wearer of the uraeus into sacred knowledge. Awe of her struck the hearts of "those whose souls were made perfect." The Wadjet, or fire-spitting cobra, represented the healing eye of the Goddess.
>
> —Normandi Ellis
> Feasts of Light

In July of 2000, an article about my career was published in L.A.'s *Whole Life Times Magazine*. "Dances with Snakes" was featured along with articles on two of my favorite heroines: Shirley MacLaine and Julia Butterfly Hill, the woman who sat in a tree for two years as an act of civil disobedience in order to save the redwoods from clear-cutting in Northern California. Both women had inspired me with their personal journeys. I grew up on Shirley's movies, but I also related to her as a dancer seeking spiritual growth. Julia's ability to put her passion into direct action reminded me of my political dance and theatre days when I toured with the Portable Theatre Company in Canada, performing environmental musical theatre.

Soon after the article was released, I received a call from a producer for a television show called *Ripley's Believe it or Not*. She explained that the show featured people who are unusual in some way, and she was interested in producing a five-minute segment on my role with the Goddess and the snakes. She thought it was extraordinary that a housewife and PTA mom danced with snakes, did yoga, and ordained women as Snake Priestesses.

I was skeptical at first, not willing to risk the humiliation of being distorted and misrepresented by the media, especially around women's issues. Once I had been interviewed and filmed with some students for a television series in Canada called *W-5*, a kind of Canadian *60 Minutes*. After hours and hours of shooting, we were horrified to see ourselves in a three minute segment displayed as goofy, over-the-edge women, prey to a strange cult. I didn't want *Ripley's* to be a repeat performance. The calling of the Goddess had to be presented with the spiritual integrity and intelligence it embodied.

Women's work has often been trivialized and scorned. Julia Butterfly Hill was ridiculed at first, even by the very movement that she was part of, until they realized that the media attention might actually be a boon for their cause. While I wasn't performing such heroic feats as Julia, I pondered whether the media could act in my favor. Perhaps a five-minute feature on *Snake Yoga* and *Dancing with Temple Serpents* would help women spark a relationship with their wild, instinctive, creative natures.

Still, doubt hovered about me like a black cloud, seizing on a core wound, my fear that I would never be seen and received by the world. At the same time, I felt determined that my gifts as a visionary sacred dancer and teacher be revealed in the light. I like to think of myself as a "cultural creative," one of many people creating new culture. But would a national audience see it the same way? Was this a chance to make a breakthrough?

I spoke to a publicist who saw it as an opportunity to get myself into the public eye. She convinced me that I could have a directorial hand in it, making it a worthwhile venue. After much internal debate, I decided to embrace the unknown and go for it. My husband stayed up nights to splice together video clips of my various dances, along with a few impromptu shots of me at home with the snakes. My assistant and I put together a press kit that the producer could use to pitch to her executive producer. Simultaneously, I toiled to make my garden and home impeccably beautiful. It took a lot of time and energy, not to mention money. I visualized myself choreographing the entire shoot, being interviewed outside by my serpent statue, teaching women yoga in my studio, and dancing with snakes. The preparations were complete. As we waited to hear back, my friends and I prayed to Divine Mother for her protection and a successful outcome.

Summer was just heating up and there were more adventures on the horizon. The season of sun was busy, indeed! As promotion for the upcoming *Finding the Inner Serpent* retreat that fall, I scheduled several *Sacred Serpent Slide Show* talks at various bookstores in Northern and Southern California. Over the years, I have collected images from many cultures worldwide on the subject of serpents. From the secular to the sacred, from children's art to photographs of women and snakes, from ancient to modern times, these images are profoundly stunning and mystical. They reflect the serpent as a symbol of healing, regeneration, immortality, and wisdom.

One of my favorite images in this presentation was the Egyptian Goddess Wadjet, also known as *Uraeus*. The *uraeus* snake appears as a cobra in every period of Egyptian art history.

Seen as a divine symbol of female beneficence and protection, it is a fundamental part of royal Egyptian art and architecture, as well as the regalia worn by deities, queens, and kings. Sally B. Johnson, author of *The Cobra Goddess of Ancient Egypt* states, "…the cobra became female power personified—the might that was used to protect gods against formlessness in the abyss of chaos and kings against evil enemies in the created world." Cobra, it seemed, was calling me.

In the middle of summer, I attended an Egyptian Mysteries weekend in Eugene, Oregon with Nicki Scully. She had become a friend and guide to me. For several years I had done both private Alchemical Healing sessions and performances with Nicki. Élan and I danced the God Horus and Goddess Hathor to her beautiful guided meditation piece on the divine lovers. Nicki had also seen some of my snake dances, so it was no surprise when she asked me to personify the Goddess Wadjet in our ritual to the Egyptian Neters. I spent part of the first evening writing my invocation and imagining how I could embody such a powerful deity. I wanted to bring her fully alive in a modern context, to give meaning to her in a way that would touch me and bless my sisters, too.

The next morning, about twenty of us gathered in Nicki's spectacular garden, each clad in ceremonial garments, ready to invoke the deities assigned to us. I wore a purple crepe-silk caftan with a hand-painted red snake circling over my belly and up toward my heart. Nearly bursting with *Shakti-Kundalini*, I stepped barefoot onto the soft green earth. An inner knowing told me that this rite would sustain my work with the serpent, spiraling its magic into my life for years to come.

The pond was chosen as the perfect place to sanctify the Goddess' presence. Nicki said that Wadjet dwelled in a secret spot among the tall papyrus reeds that rose from the water. The setting was lush, and with the summer heat, I easily drifted into another time and place, another dimension, a parallel universe.

~

I stand on the banks of the Nile River in ancient Egypt, a royal priestess performing my duties—offering oblation to the Goddess Wadjet—thanking her for fertility of the land and the people and for her protection. My body sways as the inner serpent shoots up my spine. I give way to the presence of the Goddess filling me. I chant:

> I am the fire spitting Cobra Goddess Wadjet.
> I am a woman with the head of a snake.
> I am the royal cobra also known as Buto or Edjo.
> I am the Uraeus worn on the third eye and the crown of many Egyptian deities.
> Sometimes I am worshipped as the winged cobra.
> I am the protectress of Isis and Horus.
> I am the fourteen headed cobra crown of Hathor.
> I am the spitting eye of Ra.
> I am the eye of Horus—the eye that heals—the eye that sees in both directions.
> I am Neith, the golden-headed cobra Goddess of weaving.
> I am the green fertile energy of earth.
> I am the Nile.
> I am Wadjet.

~

As I spoke the invocation, my arms, hands, and fingers made the words come to life with *mudras* and sign language. Wadjet's snake magic coursed through me. Her energy poured from my limbs as I gestured to the earth, the sky, the water and the people. The serpent Goddess had arisen in me, filling me with fire, crowning me with her *uraeus*. Swept up with the intensity I summoned the other women to the dance. We wove wildly around two drummers passionately pounding out rhythms. And we raised waves of sound with our jubilant voices. Blessings were upon us.

Weeks later, after I returned from Oregon, the call from the TV show finally came. The executive producer of *Ripley's Believe it or Not* had decided that I was not "unbelievable enough."

I was very disappointed but also relieved. My publicist, friends, and even my spiritual teachers laughed at the outcome. Perhaps Divine Mother, as trickster, had played a joke on all of us. Or maybe she portended that my life's work would be run through the mud by a media heyday and had proffered me a blessing in disguise. It was a humbling revelation, and though I couldn't know the forces at play, I knew enough to trust her wisdom.

The Cobra Goddess's guidance and protection had emanated through me for my highest good in the midst of a creative crisis. Like all the deities I've danced, she left a part of Herself with me. The very nature of Wadjet with her watchful eye and fiery force of creativity now blazed inside me.

22

A Day in the Life of a Dancing Snake Priestess

Saturday morning came too soon. I overslept and was due at the Health and Harmony Fair in Santa Rosa in two hours for a performance with my friend, Dhyanis. Dragging myself out of bed, I splashed water on my face and made breakfast. Meanwhile, my son played a game of Power Goo, turning the President's face into a monster.

I dressed quickly and applied my snake face. The black eyeliner went smoothly over my eyebrows, extending to my temples in one long stroke and disappearing into my hairline. I added another line under the bottom lid. Pearly-brown eye shadow highlighted my snake eyes.

Putting on make-up before a show usually helped to center me, but today, my nerves felt jangled. The push of time weighed heavily on my already tight shoulders. I darted about the house, gathering costumes, props, and brochures. At last, I was ready.

My son was in a chipper mood, happy to spend the day with Mom at the fair because he knew that after my performance, he'd be able to have some fun. His loving sense of cooperation helped ease my tension.

We jumped into the car. My performance in the Goddess Temple was scheduled for 2:30, and it was already 1:00. I had never been to the Santa Rosa Fairgrounds before. It was at least an hour drive away, and I still had to find the stage area and change into my costume.

I slipped the music for my performance into the tape player and listened, relaxing for a moment. The stress soon returned.

"Oh my God!" I exclaimed. "I'm featured as a dancing Snake Priestess, and I forgot the snakes!" The first crack in my "wanna-be-super-woman" veneer began to spread.

At the nearest exit, I turned the car around. Back at the house, with the car running in the driveway, I told my son to stay put while I collected my snakes. I wrapped them in a sweater and put them in a Kenyan bag. Out the door again, I flew into the car, screeched out of the driveway, and sped down the freeway until I hit bumper-to-bumper traffic on the outskirts of Santa Rosa.

"Goddess, please help me get there!" I prayed.

When we got to the fairgrounds, the parking lot was full. We found a spot, two blocks away. I barked at my son to help me gather my costumes and the snakes. He assisted me like a little gentleman. At the gate, I realized I had lost my passes to get in.

"I'm a performer, due on stage in ten minutes!" I cried.

The lady behind the window sent me to a table to get a pass.

"Whew, thank you, Goddess," I said out loud.

Running through the fair, booth after booth, I tried to figure out where I belonged. I started to cry like a lost little girl. My son squeezed my hand and said, "It will be okay, Mommy. It's okay." A rush of love and compassion came from him. Something was right with the world.

At last, I spotted the Goddess Temple and rushed into the outdoor dressing room backstage. Dhyanis was ready to go on stage. I was still crying, hoping my make-up wasn't running while copiously apologizing to her as I rummaged through my bag in search of my music. Of course, I had left it in the car. Unbelievable! Dhyanis tried to convince Liam to run back to the car and retrieve it while I changed into my costume. But he was frightened, and I knew he was too young for such a challenge. I blasted off, running past Felicity Artemis Flowers, a Dianic priestess and emcee for the show, blurting out that I would be right back.

I ran harder and faster than I had in years. My heart burned in my chest, and my toes developed blisters. But I was in the Goddess's good grace, and they held the show for me. After giving cues to the sound technician, I dashed backstage to change just as Dhyanis, in her mask as Erishkigal, brushed past me to go on stage. There was only five minutes left to pull on my tight snakeskin suit and clip on the hairpiece. As she came off stage, I wrapped the snakes around my body and rattled off directions to the stage manager for placement of my prop—a large snakeskin.

Lamia has become one of my trademark dances. The Libyan Goddess, depicted as a serpent with a woman's head, was worshipped by different names throughout the Mediterranean. She is considered a dark Goddess with attributes similar to Kali or Medusa. Thank goodness I didn't have to smile for this piece. It is a moving meditation, a shamanic journey.

∼

I sit down in my place as the music begins. It is the first time I have relaxed today, an odd sort of contradiction, all this rushing around for a seven-minute piece. After this contracted state, I am finally able to expand. I breathe into my spine and move my consciousness into my bones. I feel my vertebrae undulate the deep muscles in my belly and turn to face the crowd.

The wind blows against my face as I focus beyond the audience into the distant surrounding hills of the California wine country. Following my in-breath and out-breath, gratitude washes over me. I send out a silent prayer of thanks to Dhyanis, Felicity, the sound technician, the lady at the box office, and my son, who sits under the tent, watching the performance. All these people held space quietly supporting me as I fell apart and pieced myself back together, enabling me to walk out onto the stage with composure.

Surrounded by the protection and guidance of the Goddess, I feel my spirit lift out of my body. As if in a time warp, I drift back to my youth in the desert of New Mexico where I learned to will my spirit to soar on the winds in a turquoise sky filled with giant white thunderheads. The red rocks that rose up to touch my feet taught me how to send a grounding cord deep down into the earth. This holds me safely as I journey through time and space, back to ancient lands—Mesopotamia, Sumeria, Babylon, Egypt. I am Serpent.

For these seven minutes, I open my being as a channel for the sacred serpent energy of all time to fill my vessel. I am primordial source energy. I am the Spiral of Life.

The dance goes well even though a gust of wind almost blows the snakeskin away. I stand on it to keep it in place, dancing in one spot until I pick it up and spiral myself up in it, exiting as the long tail trails behind me. My snakes slowly and sensuously move on me. First, clinging to my neck and waist like a living necklace and belt and then entwining themselves around my arms and legs like bracelets and anklets. Their tawny shades of tan and brown blend into my costume, and we merge. Moving patterns and shapes create a living *mandala* of earth magic, guiding the viewers into the spirit of the serpent.

~

Dhyanis nodded at me in approval as we passed each other again, she, on her way to the stage as *Kali* this time and me, to change into the *Celtic Woman* costume. I was glad to shed my skin and don a more comfortable costume. My black velvet bodice with its long, flowing chiffon skirt and a full-length black cape with a hood, add a sense of mystery of the night. Through sign language and modern dance, it expresses the soulful quality of my nature.

Celtic Woman danced to Loreena McKennitt's, "Dark Night of the Soul" is one of my favorite pieces to perform. Loreena sings a love poem as exquisite as any of Rumi's poetry, weaving in the words of St. John of the Cross, a Christian Sufi mystic of 15th century Spain. My Irish Catholic woman-girl-child self is honored in this piece. I feel as if I am merging with Jesus on the night before his crucifixion, kneeling in the Garden of Gesthemane outside his Beloved Mary Magdelena's home. The passion and sensuality in this dance reveal an intoxicating union of the divine lovers within the self and the intrinsic longing within us all to be met by another on this plane, one that Rumi so deliciously delves into in his relationship with Shams. In the six minutes and forty-five seconds of this dance, I am mystically transformed into the Love, Lover, Beloved that I ache for in the most intimate passageways of the self.

It was a relief to dance this prayer on an open-air stage for the gods and goddesses, the young and old hippies, and new moms with their babies asleep in their slings.

My dances are prayers that humanity can be restored to the Beauty Way. By witnessing the power of a woman exuding a sensuality that is real and full of spirit, earthly divinity becomes possible for all of us. Jesus knew this, just as surely as the spirit in my body knows that the veil of the belly dancer is a transcendent expression of the veil of the nun that I once wanted to wear as a young Catholic schoolgirl.

In ecstatic reverie, I changed back into my street clothes in the dressing room and returned to my masquerade as an American housewife and Mom, prepared to indulge my son in wispy cotton candy and other mainstream junk in abundance at the fair.

Liam went on a giant blow-up slide replica of the sinking Titanic at least five times while I sat on a bench in a meditative state. With a Mona Lisa smile on my face, I pretended to enjoy his revelry. After an excursion of climbing and rappelling a fake mountain and having his photo taken while at the top, Liam told me he was hungry. We ate a healthy lunch at a vegan raw foods booth and left.

Back on the freeway, we enjoyed some of that much-needed golden silence that all the money in the world can't buy.

At home, Liam played with a friend while I prepared for the evening's belly-gram to the PTA President's husband. My services had been donated to the school auction. Here was my chance to blow my cover as "mere Mom" and blow their minds at the same time.

Refreshing my stale make-up, I added glitter to my face, throat, belly, and arms, parted my blonde locks with a comb, and snapped pastel butterfly clips around the crown of my head that matched the butterfly belly dance costume. I donned a full, royal purple velvet vest over the costume and slipped my feet into turquoise sequined slippers. And off I went.

There were several cars in the driveway of the Marin hillside house, and there wasn't enough room for me to park. I was backing down the hill when the wheels on the left side of the vehicle went over the curb and got stuck.

"Merde," I said under my breath. "Shit," in French, is also the dancer's way of saying good luck before a performance.

My Italian host, Frank Spumoni, met me at the door. I handed him my music tape as his wife ushered me into a bathroom to hide.

These upwardly mobile folks waited in an elegant living room with plush white carpeting, seated on white leather couches, drinking martinis. When the music began, I strode into the room, hips swaying, furiously playing my finger cymbals, a sultry smile upon my lips and headed directly to the guest of honor. Dick was appropriately surprised. He played the seduction game with finesse as I pranced around him, pretending he was my boy toy. Male egos love this, and I must admit, so do I.

Unwrapping the turquoise, rainbow-sequined silk veil, I spun around, creating spirals and butterfly wings. With my mouth and nose covered Arabian style, I slid my eyes from side to side.

The children snuck in and watched, wide-eyed. A little boy asked, "Are you Liam's mommy?"

"Yes," I answered proudly.

The child's sweetness melted everyone's reserve. Under my breath, I chuckled to myself, recalling that after one of my Goddess dance concerts in Toronto, Liam's godfather announced to my son, "Some kids have PTA moms. You got lucky."

Grabbing the veil tautly between two fists, I addressed Dick's wife. "What shall we do with him?"

"Whatever he wants. It's his birthday!"

Dick chimed in, "Tie me up. Tie me up!"

We all joked that it needed to be G-rated for the kids.

The guests were intrigued. I lingered awhile, the suspense building. Immersed in my own little world of shimmies and belly rolls, I was totally full of myself. Then I threw the veil around Dick's hips and challenged him to match my shimmying hips and undulating belly. He dutifully obliged.

Everyone was laughing harder now so I zeroed in on the finale. I perched on the edge of his chair and commanded him to entertain me. He pulled a fast one on all of us, quickly grabbing the chair with me in it as if he was going to lug me off to the bedroom.

"Thanks, guys. We'll see you later," he joked.

I was impressed with his strength. As he put me down, I took my bow and paraded down the hallway to the door.

It was both embarrassing and funny to ask for help with my car. Frank and Dick volunteered, but the car was so jammed that I had to call AAA.

As I walked back into the house to use the phone, Dick asked, "What do you really do?"

I told him I was writing a book about snakes.

"Oh, you mean it's about me? I'm a lawyer."

The party guests cruised off in their BMWs, Lexuses, and Mercedes to a four-star restaurant for dinner. I stood in the driveway in full belly dance regalia—sparkle shoes and all—waiting for the AAA tow truck to arrive.

Gypsy Dance

Lamia

23

Snake Bite

Snake medicine people are very rare. Their initiation involves experiencing and living through multiple snake bites, which allows them to transmute all poisons, be they mental, physical, spiritual, or emotional. The power of snake medicine is the power of creation, for it embodies sexuality, psychic energy, alchemy, reproduction, and ascension (or immortality).

—Jamie Sams and David Carson
Medicine Cards:
The Discovery of Power Through the Ways of Animals

Oh Emerald Tree Boa
Green Snake
Green Goddess
Fertile Mistress of Mysteries
You of the Seven Coils
You of the Seven Chakras
You of the Seven Sacred Seals
Come awaken me
Come ignite me with your strike

—Le'ema

Hunger Bite

You can't be a true snake keeper without having been bitten. And the lessons that come with snakebites never cease to stupefy even a Snake Priestess.

One morning, when Isis, my boa constrictor, was a baby, she mistook me for food. Fortunately, I knew my pets' bites were not venomous. The bite didn't hurt; in fact, I laughed out loud at her wild, ferocious behavior, cleaned off the blood, and went about my business.

A few months went by, and seemingly for no reason, my ring finger swelled up and turned red. When I went to the doctor, she said it looked like a splinter and gave me a homeopathic remedy of *Silica*. Since I had been gardening, I assumed she was right and took the remedy. The redness and swelling disappeared, and I forgot about it again.

Weeks later, my finger felt a bit itchy. Pinching it, I noticed the tiniest puncture hole and figured it itched because it was healing. But the more it itched, the more I scratched, and the more I scratched, the more it itched. I must have scratched that itch all day long.

Finally, I squeezed it hard between my thumb and index finger as if I was popping a pimple. Sure enough, a big glob of puss oozed out. I thought that would fix it. Then I noticed something that resembled a splinter would appear each time I squeezed it, disappearing when I stopped. Bound and determined to remove the splinter, I asked my husband for help. After several tries with the tweezers, he gripped the tiny white thing, pulled it out, and dropped it into his palm.

It resembled a cat's claw; but it was no cat's claw. We wondered what the hell it was. We leaned in close and gasped with amazement. It was an entire little snake fang!

Three months had passed since Isis had bit me. Now, having had an embedded snake fang lodged inside my ring finger, I was truly initiated into the clan of the snake keepers.

Hormone Bite

Another time, I received a bite from my python, Nidaba. This time it was an angry bite, an instinctual way of saying "You piss me off. Stay out of my space." I wasn't that surprised. After all, I'd been feeling angry for days and had been unable to move it out of my body in a constructive way. Perhaps my irritation had transferred to her.

The blood—pulsing scarlet pearls of life force—sprang up in two tiny pools in the soft-webbed flesh between the thumb and index finger of my right hand. I paused in my ordinary reality to contemplate the extraordinary message here. Wake up! Acupuncture via fangs equals Snake Medicine.

For the past month, I'd been like a snake digesting a big meal, unable to move, much less write. A contracted inward spiraling time into myself had followed an expansive time of teaching two retreats. During both of these workshops, only a couple of weeks apart, I had been menstruating. Menses was normally a time of hibernation for me. Now, I was being challenged to hold an outward focus while my body was longing to stay in the looks-within space. Two periods in one month? Peri-menopausal upheaval. The Goddess was having her way with me, and there was nothing I could do but surrender.

Nidaba bit me when she was "in the blue," a time when the old skin, like an opaque milky blue cocoon, is about to be shed. As a menstruating woman, I was not operating out of the frontal thinking, neo-cortex part of my brain but was pulled back into the instinctual, primal rhythm of the reptilian brain. Science has described the human brain as comprised of three parts with increasing evolutionary sophistication: the reptilian brain, the mammalian brain, and the neo-cortex. The reptilian brain is located at the back of the brain, which sits on top of our spinal column and controls basic functions such as breathing, digestion, and excretion. Hormones involve primarily the reptilian brain.

Externally, it looked like a simple snakebite—one of the hazards of the "job." Internally, it was about the unexpressed anger and inability to attend to my personal needs. My doctor recognized this and prescribed *Lachesis*, a remedy made from the venom of the South American Bushmaster. It is used as a key remedy for sensitive and passionate women with PMS.

During menstruation my whole being wanted to stay still in a dark quiet space. I didn't want to be disturbed until the old skin, the lining of my uterus, was fully shed. Then I could emerge, slithering like a snake out of its old casing in a silken, shiny skin, smoothly sculpting a new path in the wet clay earth.

Holy Bite

The seventh snakebite, the worst I've ever received, was at a dance event on Samhain in 2007. I was asked to perform with my snake for the finale of the show and afterwards lead a ritual spiral dance with the cast and the audience.

Two women had fought in the dressing room where my boa, Isis, was tucked in her basket in the corner. Once again, it seemed my sensitive snake had contracted the hostile energy in the space. When I came to gather her up for our dance and gently removed her covering, she jabbed her jaws into my left forearm and constricted tightly. I was taken aback and frightened. She wouldn't release her grip, and I had to pull her off. This left a gaping wound that gushed blood. There were only two minutes before I had to go on stage, but the bite was serious, and I needed help fast.

Snake Bite

I motioned to a couple of dancers who were watching from the wings. One held my arm still, applying pressure above the wound, while the other cleaned it off quickly and applied antiseptic and a bandage. A third dancer standing nearby placed her snake bracelet over the bandage to hold it in place in an empowering gesture of sisterhood.

The music started. There is nothing like the "ever present Now" of being on stage that forces one to be completely in the moment. This time it was even more intense. I walked on stage in a composed manner, yet in an extremely altered and alert state, a Goddess-embodied trance. Often I choreographed my dances, but this time the serpent came through me, weaving the chaotic energies into reverence. Slow, dreamy music soothed the audience and Isis calmed. The dance poured out of my body with surprising physical strength, from my legs, through my belly, and out through my heart. No one noticed my injured arm.

The serpent's bite opened me to the fullness of my role as priestess. Ancient priestesses learned their particular function as part of the snakebite initiation. What the serpent chose to teach, the priestess learned to offer to others. I understood immediately that I was to hold soft, wise feminine energy and spread it throughout the group—smoothing the profane atmosphere into sacred space. To bring the people together in ceremony required this grounding and centering of the priestess.

We were now ready to invite our ancestors to join us. The voice of the snake came through me low, deep and strong: "Tonight is a special night. The veil between the worlds is thin, allowing us to make contact with our beloved dead. They are happy to be with us and want to help us fulfill the dream of the people. Touch the floor and speak their names. Ask them for help in your lives. Now we shall dance on the heads of our ancestors."

Everyone touched the floor, calling in the ancestors. Then we flowed into a spiral dance while looking into each other's eyes, and sang: "Spiraling into the center, the center of the wheel, I am a weaver, I am the woven one, I am a dreamer, I am the dream."

The bite was not so easily healed this time. Since I was leaving for Egypt in five days, I saw my homeopath. She explained how to care for the wound and informed me that it was not an accident. It was a "Holy Act." It needed to happen before the trip to help me stand strong in the face of adversity. She gave me a new snake venom remedy, *Viper*!

After boarding the plane with my arm wrapped up, I opened a book, *The Mysteries of Isis*, by DeTraci Regula. In it, she recounts the story of Ra, the Sun God, who has grown old and incompetent:

> Isis decides that she cannot allow the destruction of the universe to occur and becomes determined to obtain the Secret Name of Ra, the supreme word of power, which will allow her to heal him and to also be able to rule in his place if necessary.

She fashions a serpent out of the mud formed by the spittle of Ra. When the great serpent bites him, she offers to save his life if he will reveal his secret name, the source of his power. With the exchange in place, she chants his name to heal him so that he may continue his path through the heavens.

As the plane circled over the pyramids in the land of the Goddess Isis, I looked out the window and then at the wound on my arm, and realized that even she healed through the bite of the serpent.

I wondered was the bite on my arm prophetic, reminding me, as a priestess, to make myself available for the personal transformation of others?

24

Snake Venom

> The cross-cultural archetype of woman-and-snake is older than time, linking biological femaleness to the transformative and regenerative qualities of the undulating snake who regularly sheds its skin.
>
> —Vicki Noble
> Uncoiling the Snake,
> Ancient Patterns in Contemporary Women's Lives

The two-inch silver snakes dangling from my ears caught the eye of my observant homeopathic doctor.

"Are those cobras?" she asked. A multitude of black braids spiraled past the shoulders of her flowing white gown.

The unique earrings were a gift to me from one of my priestesses who claimed they were too intense for her to wear as an RN in labor and delivery at the local hospital. I had once admired them, and later, after her ordination ceremony, she dropped them in my palm and said they belonged to me.

The Eustachian tubes in my ears had been clogged up for over a month, causing significant hearing loss and pain. I complained to the doctor not only about the symptoms I was experiencing, but also the menopausal uproar raging through my body. PMS and heavy periods had left me nearly incapacitated.

The strong Nigerian woman's eyes pierced me with a powerful, organic knowing. "Give me a moment," she said, leaving the room.

Rage and grief stirred in me again. I had felt angry for over a month, using every curse word in the book. My behavior was toxic. Everything from men to the government—made up mostly of men—pissed me off.

When she returned, the doctor handed me a small, brown envelope. It had the word *Naja* scrawled in her snaky script on the front. *Naja*, cobra venom! In ancient Egypt, cobras were revered as the symbol of life and immortality; in India and other Hindu cultures, they are still considered sacred.

"I want you to take this remedy for one week and then come back for a stronger potency," she told me. "The lower potency will work on the physical, and the higher potency will work on the emotional and spiritual levels."

She explained that snake venom remedies are often used to treat menopausal symptoms, but they can help with other concerns as well. "People who benefit from *Naja* tend to be romantic in nature and highly devoted to their families, but they are also emotionally sensitive and will often erupt without warning. They tend to sulk at perceived injustices and can even become suicidal."

It was as if she had looked right into my psyche. Desperate for relief, I put three pellets of the homeopathic venom under my tongue and sucked hard, waiting for transformation.

Instantly, my ears drained, and the mucus moved down my throat. My consciousness slid out of ordinary reality, and I transformed into the revered snake of the Far East. My hood fanned open, and my spine arched as I curved up through my chest, lifting my head high in alert, poised to strike. I felt venom sacs in place of my human ears, and my tongue twitched, ready to spit poison.

I remembered hearing a lecture on how shamans fully become their totem animal, seeing and feeling through the animal in order to embody the medicine of that creature. Here I was again, becoming the snake, but this time, the Cobra—a large snake identified by its hood, an appendage of skin and muscle that flares in the presence of predators.

I walked out of the doctor's office in a completely shape-shifted state. As I got into the car, I laughed out loud like a crazy woman. *If only people could see the snake woman driving a car!* I felt strong and awake with the power of my womanhood and yet very child-like, playful, and innocent.

As I passed by a second-hand clothing shop, I found myself turning the car around and pulling into the parking lot. To my delight, there was a dress with a snake design on it, just waiting for me. I pulled it off the rack and navigated to the back of the store, through the dingy aisles of funky stuff, to a simple dressing room. I quickly shed my clothes and tried on the snake dress. It fit perfectly. The soft satin fabric had the same markings and color as the cobra and the cool, smoothness of a snake's skin. The back's diamond-shaped cutout bared my shoulder blades. My trapezius muscles made the same U-shaped pattern that appears on the back of the Cobra's hood when it's fanned open. My rib cage looked like a snake's spine with its numerous floating ribs attached to a strong backbone. Yes, this was a definitive must for my growing wardrobe of serpent attire!

After changing back into my street clothes, I slithered up to the cash register to purchase the dress, a wily snake smile on my face. Back in the car, I chanted at full volume a song I had learned from Starhawk: "Snakewoman shedding her skin, shedding, shedding, shedding her skin."

At home, I pulled my pythons out of their cage where they had been soaking in a bowl of warm water and placed them in separate baskets so they wouldn't fight over the food. I gave them each a mouse and closed the lid of the baskets.

Upon returning to check on them, I noticed that the skin of one of my snakes hung limp around its body. In all my years of raising snakes, I had never seen this exact moment before. The entire skin was ready to be shed. Tingling with excitement, I gently lifted the snake from the basket, careful not to disturb her. I rolled the skin down her long slender body as though taking off a sock from the inside out. To my surprise, the skin came off in one, continuous piece. Mother Nature's miracle! This was the first time my python had experienced an intact shed. Perhaps this was a sign that I, too, would shed the layers of old skins that prevented me from fully healing.

I thought about how, in my Snake Priestess retreats, we do a *Shedding Our Old Skin Ritual* in which the woman can viscerally feel her old skins being removed through the use of layers of silk veils. First, women are given exercises that explore the ways they are stuck by using the metaphor of the Medusa turning us to stone through our emotional blocks. Then they learn a variation of the *Fire Breath Orgasm*, a process in which breath and energy circulate through the chakras as a way to release blockages and raise *Kundalini* for personal and planetary healing.

Ambient music, wafting incense, candlelight, and the sentient presence of each woman create an ancient temple atmosphere where deep levels of healing can take place. Several priestesses place veils upon a receptive woman as she lies in a gestative state. Two or more women hold the ends in their hands and work in unison, dancing to give life to the veils. They float softly over the initiate's body.

Once the veils are in place, they are then removed one by one, sliding over her naked body as if they are layers of skin being pulled off, shedding effortlessly. When the final silk veil, painted as the rainbow serpent, lifts from the face and body, a newborn sheen emanates from the initiate. She is lifted up, held, and kissed by her sisters as we affirm to her, "Thou art born anew." It is one of my favorite ritual enactments to give and receive.

How I longed for the ability to let go of worn out ways and habits that no longer served me. I desired a thorough healing, a full shedding of the old and the past. Perhaps the intact shed was a sign that I could have an easier journey into menopause.

They say the measure of good health for a snake is how well it sheds its skin. No wonder their unique ability to regenerate three or more times each year makes them a universal symbol of transformation and healing.

I didn't know it would be many more moons before my monthly cycles would end. But with each dose of *Naja* Cobra venom, the difficult symptoms eased. What a perfect remedy for a Snake Priestess!

Shedding Your Old Skin Ceremony, October 2001

Le'ema as Lamia in the Desert
Photocomposition by Gentry George

25

Full Moon Snakes

The sun has set and the moon is surely rising. Grandmother Moon follows me. She stays behind me, round, full, peering over my left shoulder as I walk the moist earth in my moccasins. The streets are damp. It is a clear night between winter rainstorms in Northern California. Like a caged animal set free, I am answering the call of the wild.

The Queen of the Night, Grandmother Moon, has lured me out to make my prayers. In her majestic sky, the constellations, set free too, have come out of hiding from behind rain clouds. Orion, with his bow, is on my left, protecting me as I go. The Pleiades are high above. Grandmother Moon is guiding me, holding me, singing to me. Her songs tell me that I am open to learning more snake wisdom. Her voice inside my head seductively sings songs of remembrance, songs I've heard in lifetimes past. A *déjà vu*. A haunting, yet inviting melody, like the sounds of an ocarina, awakens pre-encoded cellular memories in me. Stored for eons in the records of the Great Spirit, this celestial music opens my being, revealing a new reality:

~

My daughter, all over the world, there are tribes of snake sisters that are your relations. In these cultures, the snakewoman tribe is represented by the snake indigenous to that part of the earth. In India, she is represented by the Cobra, in North America, she is represented by the Rattler, in South America by the Boa, in Africa by the Python, in Europe by the Adder, and in Asia the Dragon. These 'Serpents of Wisdom' are everywhere on the Earth Mother since time immemorial. You are part of this vast web of life awakening at this critical time to the wisdom of these ancients. You are your ancestors, my child. You are indeed a Snake Priestess. The Pleiades are your tribal sisters in this galaxy. They are the Seven Snake Sisters.

~

Refreshed from my brisk walk, I arrived back home feeling gratitude and a sense of purpose in being part of a grander scope of life. I knew in my bones that this gift of Grandmother Moon's communication to me was real. Yet, my rational side wanted proof. The inner critic swiftly took over.

The sweet communion with spirit I experienced under the moonlight slipped from my consciousness as I immersed myself in the task of cooking a meal and eating it while watching a kid movie with my son.

Later, I lay in bed with my favorite book on the history, mythology, and spiritual lineages of the serpent masters around the world. *The Return of the Serpents of Wisdom* by Mark Amaru Pinkham is an exquisite exposition of ancient mysteries surrounding the Serpent. The book fell open to a section on the Pleiades. My jaw dropped open as I read:

> *Our serpent creator is the seven sisters, the Pleiades.*
>
> The seven aspects of the Primal Serpent Creator were anciently worshipped in the heavens as the seven stars of the Pleiades. The Mayans paid homage to the Pleiades as a manifestation of the great Celestial Serpent. The Greek Gnostics referred to the star group as the 'seven pillars' of Sofia, their Serpent Creatress...embodiment of the 'wisdom of God'. In the Bible, the Pleiades are represented as the seven creative stars in the right hand, the creative hand, of God.

My spine tingled, and the hairs on my body stood on end. Oh, my Goddess! Epiphany! The many threads in my consciousness came together, weaving themselves into a tapestry of understanding. Things started lining up, and I saw how my research on various Snake Goddesses and the intuitive track I had followed for the last ten years were in sync.

There is a Roman Goddess called Dea Syria. She is encircled with seven coils of a great serpent, and her head emerges from the serpent's mouth. There are seven eggs tucked between the serpent's coils and her body. Of course, it all makes perfect sense now. The dance of the seven veils, the seven chakras, the seven sacraments, and now, the seven snake sisters! Even the word S E R P E N T has seven letters in it. My moonstruck madness must have had much truth to it. Eagerly I flipped through a few more pages to read:

> *The moon is a secondary source of serpent life force coming to the earth.*
>
> The Serpent life force was also believed to emanate from the Moon, especially during the waxing and full Moon. In Egypt, the Moon and

its rays were associated with the Gods Seth and Thoth-Hermes, both of whom were intimately associated with the Primal Dragon and the serpent/life force. In Europe, the Moon was consistently associated with the Dragon, especially within the paganistic nature cults. In India, the Moon and its rays was often associated with the Serpent Goddess Shakti and the Dragon Goddess Kali...

Grandmother Moon's guidance was divine indeed. How could I have doubted the revelation her pristine presence gave me? In the brief time of my walk, the moon had provided sustaining nourishment for my spiritual essence. I continued to read heartily, devouring the next few pages like the most exquisite gourmet food I had ever tasted. For dessert, I capped it off with this:

The preserving life force also arrives to earth from the Pleiades, the celestial serpent.

The Ancients also recognized the point of creation in our local galaxy, the Pleiades, to be a transmitter of preserving life force to Earth. Each spring when the Pleiades hovered above the horizon at dawn and/or reached its apex in the sky at noon, there was believed to be a fresh infusion of life force projected to Earth through the 'teats of the rattlesnake' This annual infusion of cosmic energy manifested on Earth as the nourishing spring rains and the activating spark which stimulated the growth of new vegetation...

I closed the book and fell into a deep sleep with energy spirals dancing all around me. My body felt like it contained the magnetic mystery of planets and galaxies spinning within me. My dreams had a quality of things stirring, a stirring of the inner cauldron, the black, velvet void, where beauteous truths float in the streams of my beingness. I dreamed I was the shape and structure of DNA itself, a double-helix spiral. I became the twin serpents intertwining themselves around my spine. My chakras were luminously pulsating with their shapes of sacred geometry as I dwelled in this dark state of light.

I woke up longing for the moon. A whole day had to pass before I could be out under her opalescent rays again. Still in a trance, I got my son off to school. Then I took a ballet class feeling the stiffness of my joints, but appreciating the live classical music of the piano. The sweetness of the music was soothing. Going through the motions of the ballet *barre*, I was still under the moon's spell.

I made my way through a gorgeous sunny day running errands, in anticipation of the night. All I could think about is the moon. Not only was it a full moon, it was a month before the Spring Equinox. There was a quickening in the air. The hills were glowing emerald green, and the daffodils and narcissus were already poking their sweet heads out of the earth. It was not quite warm enough yet for the snakes to be out of hibernation.

Years ago in late spring, I had taken a walk with Liam and a friend in this area during an unusual hot spell. A baby snake, four or five inches long, crossed our path, and I reached down and gently picked it up. Holding it in the palms of my hands for my young son and his friend to see, I was stroking it and cooing to it, when I noticed it was a rattlesnake. I counted seven rattles! It was so tiny I didn't think it could be harmful and continued communing with it, holding it close to our faces for a better view.

Some time later, however, a herpetologist informed me that young rattlesnakes are more dangerous than fully grown ones because the older ones know how to ration their poison, whereas the young ones usually strike using all their venom at once. I was astonished to hear this. The practice of *Ahimsa*, kindness to all living creatures, served us well that day when I held the baby snake. I will never know whether it was truly dangerous or not, but I will probably never pick up a rattlesnake again. Now I see that Rattlesnake was showing itself to me yet again as my medicine totem.

Brooke Medicine Eagle tells a story about a large grandmother rattler she encountered in the countryside near Austin, Texas. She was following the natural flows of water lines on the land, also known as dragon lines, when a big snake reared its head. Fiercely shaking her rattles and hissing, Grandmother Rattler let them know she was near. Brooke knew she wouldn't strike but that the snake had come as a messenger. Brooke communed with her, looking her straight in the eyes. Grandmother Rattler revealed the importance of these dragon lines. Curvy dragon lines or water lines are yin in character, and help to keep the balance of feminine energy on the earth.

According to Alex Champion, "Often these water veins cross with energy leys or *ley lines*. They are yang in character and straight as an arrow, in contrast to water lines...Energy leys are also found at stone circles, and where they cross with water veins, they form what dowsers call power spots." Mystics all over the world have known about the energy of power spots for thousands of years.

It is understood that when the earth is pierced in these power spots with a stone or an obelisk that the power of the earth pours out and is available to the people for transformation and healing. Stonehenge is such an example. Perhaps the legends of dragon slayers as heroes are really metaphors about finding power spots and tapping into that energy, the serpentine *Kundalini* energy of the Earth Mother Herself. Brooke Medicine Eagle sensed that Grandmother Rattler was telling her this dragon line was a power spot, a place of sacred energy to be honored and respected.

The rattlesnake is sacred to the Americas. The Milky Way is even called the Rattlesnake by the Mayans. Perhaps on my walk this evening under the moonlight, the Milky Way, the Rattlesnake in the sky, would have a message for me.

At last the end of my day drew near. I picked Liam up from school and rushed home.

"Wanna go on a full moon hike with me?"

"No, Mom, I just wanna stay home."

"Okay, but... I'll be gone for awhile."

He opted for playing video games. After setting him up with a snack, I raced out the door and drove up to the ridge. Ah, freedom at last! I reached the hills just in time to catch the last warm rays before sunset. Sunset with a full moon rise were my favorite times to be walking in nature.

For many years in the mountains of New Mexico, I practiced a sun/moon meditation that can only be experienced during the full moon rising at sunset. One has to be at a high enough point, at just the right time, to feel this exquisite moment and utilize it for healing. Standing between the setting sun and the rising moon, the polarization of male and female energies comes into balance. As I face the sun, I open my chest to the heavenly love of Father Sky and my back to the intuitive wisdom of Divine Mother. Then I turn to face Grandmother Moon, opening my heart to her milky white rays of feminine healing and my wings to the solar light of Grandfather Sun. Lifted by their light, co-joined in my body, my spirit soars in ecstatic flight during these meditations. This night I was eager to relive this experience of the sun/moon alignment.

I made my way up the hill, passing through a fragrant grove of tall eucalyptus trees. The trail was muddy and I had to avoid puddles strewn in the path. The climb, pleasantly steep, was just enough to make me breathe deeper. The air was fresh and invigorating. At the top, I paused, happy that I had made time for myself to make this journey once again, especially tonight. I tiptoed gently to my sacred spot. It was time.

The sun was setting behind Mount Tamalpais, and the moon was rising over the Richardson Bay. I stood strong upon the earth in my moccasins, feeling the bottoms of my feet open as the spirals of earth's magnetic energy traveled up my feet and legs into my body. I felt rooted. I belonged here. I closed my eyes and let the crimson-orange rays of the sun penetrate my eyelids and shine into my forehead. Smiling, I focused the sun's warm rays on my heart and the cool rays of the moon on my back between my shoulder blades. I breathed deeply and let the energies of sun, moon and earth blend inside my body.

Then, as if by magic, the door to the top of my head opened, as the Hopis say, and my spirit soared exuberantly out of my body on a long silver cord. My spirit wings fanned out, fluttering, as I watched my light body fly like the winged ones higher into the light of Grandfather Sun. I stayed this way for a long time, feeling liberated. Then slowly turning to face Grandmother Moon, my face softened. I dropped more deeply into meditation. Her platinum rays soothed me, settling me into a tranquil stillness. Grandfather Sun turned my wings golden, and I floated effortlessly above the mountains and the bay, like the hawks in the area, soaring on the air currents. Content and joyous, completely bliss filled, I gave thanks to be alive at this moment.

I turned around to say goodbye to the sun as it set. In awe and gratitude, I sat under the full moon with my back against my sacred yoni tree, an old scrub oak that had been hollowed out over the years. Like a child making sure its mother was still there, I glanced up at Grandmother Moon's silver countenance before my head slumped onto my chest. Grandmother sang me into her dream again. Drunk on moonbeams, I drifted ever more deeply into a lunar stupor, listening to her beguiling tunes as she sang sweetly to me of my destiny:

~

Through your devotion to the dance you have become the priestess you are now and have been in lifetimes past. You have served the Divine Feminine well and will continue to do so in this lifetime. I, and my starry sisters, the Pleiades, swell with pride for you. You will now be more aware of our guiding presence in your life, and we will always be available to you.

Tonight you are wondering how the seven snake sisters, the Pleiades, correlate to the many esoteric teachings you have received. Let me tell you, when you first created your dance to the Goddess *Inanna,* as the *"Dance of the Seven Veils,"* you were following our guidance. You were enacting a most ancient ritual of rituals done by priestesses. Inanna's journey was a very important teaching for you.

Let me remind you that you were forty-two years old when you performed this dance for the first time. Six times seven is forty-two. At forty-two, you had completed six steps out of the sevenfold journey of your soul. You were moving from Toronto to California at this time, where you would finish the seventh step before you reached the age of forty-nine. Forty-nine is a priestess's coming of age year when she has traversed this sevenfold journey of her soul. You have been giving this beautiful *Dance of the Seven Veils* journey to several of your sisters upon their fiftieth birthday when they have completed seven full cycles of seven years. This is part of your service in awakening other women to their souls' dance of remembrance.

We gave you this inspiration when you were forty-two, so that you could do this work and offer it to others with understanding by the time you reached the age of forty-nine. My dear one, you are well on your way. Continue to provide this ceremony to your women friends in your service as a priestess. Although you have given it to just three women as of now, soon you will have given it to seven women. The numbers will multiply and the teachings will spread. Through the language of the body, the dance, this ancient serpent wisdom of shedding the layers and awakening the seven chakras with the seven sacraments will become more apparent, and your work as a priestess will flourish.

∼

I came out of my trance with a start. The moon beamed lovingly down on me. An eternity had passed. The pink haze after sunset, the Belt of Venus, had disappeared, and the stars sparkled in a sapphire sky. I better get home, I thought, getting up in a hurry. My family must be getting hungry. I staggered down the hillside, a lunatic inebriated on an elixir of moon milk.

As I passed through the eucalyptus grove again on my way down, I looked up between the tall trees for a last lingering look at the stars and caught a glimpse of the Pleiades winking down at me. I whispered a silent prayer of gratitude to the "Seven Sisters," thanking them for their beneficent guidance and to Grandmother Moon for her constant outpouring of love and generosity to me.

I got into my car and let out a walloping "Yahoo," started up the engine, and drove down the mountain. At home, my son was still glued to his video games and my husband was glued to his cell phone. Humming with excitement, I quickly prepared dinner. When we finished eating, I left my husband and son to do the dishes and settled down at the computer to write about the evening's adventures.

My office space shares the adjoining family room and I had just begun when my son trailed in after me. Liam started to roughhouse with Élan and threw a pillow toward me. A ceramic statue of the Virgin Mary, standing on the world with the serpent at her feet, toppled to the floor and shattered.

Suddenly, something from way back in the recesses of my childhood memories came blasting through the surface of my psyche with the urgency of coming up quickly from deep waters for air. A strong vision flashed before me. There stood the Madonna, not only with the serpent at her feet, standing on the Universe, but with seven stars surrounding her head. A mystical truth, hidden in the memories of my Catholic girlhood, revealed itself to me. The Madonna, the universe, the seven stars, and the serpent were all swirling in my head like a great cosmic soup of ordered chaos. The connection of all these was what the moon, as the Goddess immanent, had shown me. I had to laugh out loud with joy. Divine Mother was truly with me.

Normally, I would have lost my temper, but this time I just stood up in amazement, my mouth gaping wide. Élan and Liam silently held their breath, waiting for my reaction. They were shocked when I laughed out loud. A few blissful elations tumbled from my mouth. They looked at me quizzically and poured out apologies. I simply stated that my son would have to replace the statue with his allowance.

I stopped writing and turned off the computer. Leaving them to pick up the pieces, I gathered my coat around my shoulders and walked outside. In the crisp night air, the presence of Ishtar, Inanna, and Salome accompanied me with Grandmother Moon.

Brooke Medicine Eagle with Le'ema on her fortieth birthday

26

Serpent Spirals of Life and Death

The shell of my baby corn snake's former self lay coiled in a perfect spiral. Pyro's new body slithered out of his old body through the orifice of the mouth. The fully intact shed with a wide toothless grin was an identical imprint of a creature gone somewhere else, leaving only papery thin remains.

It was a dark moon night with no trace of the silvery orb in the sky. Death was in the air: stillness, blackness, emptiness. It was the end of an era. Ruth, my ninety-year-old mother-in-law, died on Mother's Day in the year 2000. She passed with a smile on her face only two hours after her youngest son told her, "Mom, it's Mother's Day. It's a good day to die. We are all ready when you are, and we are with you." Like my snake, leaving his outgrown skin, Ruth wriggled free of her worn, tired body.

After many years of being angry at God for taking her husband on their sixtieth wedding anniversary, among other reasons, Ruth finally 'let go and let God.' She had never been particularly interested in her own spirituality. Instead, she had a tribal connection with Judaism. She was not, however, a religious Jew.

I had just completed a month-long yoga teacher training at a retreat center in the Sierra Foothills. It was there that I contemplated the difference between religion and spirituality. Divine Mother would come to me often in my meditations in the form of Ananda Mayi Ma, the bliss-permeated woman saint of India, known as the guru to the gurus. Ananda Mayi Ma was awakened at birth, and when she was a young woman, God spoke to her, instructing her to bow down to no one. She followed no lineage, just her own unique urging toward God and was often lost in ecstatic trance states of divine communion. One of my sister students in the Sierras would often say: "Religion is tribal, but spirituality is individual."

Lama Surya Das, an American Jewish man by birth and the most highly trained lama in the Tibetan tradition, says this of spirituality: "Walking the spiritual path brings us in touch with pure being and the truth of who we are. What a relief! Spirituality is authentic and real. Spirituality is sane, natural, meaningful living. Yes, philosophers and theologians agree: what we seek is naturally within us all."

Simply put, finding our true essence involves getting in touch with our own inner sacred core. We do this when we let go of all pretenses and stop hiding behind the various masks we create to keep ourselves under control.

Ruth's favorite word, which summed up much of her life, was "control." When my husband and I would visit, instead of asking us how we were doing, she would ask, "Is everything under control?" This would infuriate me; I found it so dehumanizing! But Ruth needed to control everyone and everything around her. Unfortunately, illness had its own agenda.

Ruth's doctor gave her a cocktail of drugs—anti-anxiety and serotonin uptake inhibitors to help her release the negative mind state. Through studies on brain function, medical science has discovered that meditation can achieve the same states of mind that medication attempts to establish. There is only one letter difference between the two words! Perhaps meditation will be the prescribed medication of the future.

It was a blessing indeed that Ruth had Alzheimer's. What better way to let go of control than to lose one's mind. Although it was difficult for her sons to watch Ruth's degeneration, her illness became her greatest ally, enabling her to achieve a personal victory on her path toward spirituality, her 'pure essence.' As she lost her mind, she found her spirit.

When Ruth finally let go of control, she also let go of paranoia and became like an innocent child seeing the world through eyes of wonder. She lost her capacity for forming thoughts and speaking words, deepening into silence—that still, small voice inside our hearts that enables us to hear and be filled with our own Holy Spirit. This is the place of true meditation.

My Mother's Day was spent with Liam, waiting and wondering when Ruth would take her final journey home. I looked at my ten-year-old son, 'the apple of my eye,' and thought someday he would be in the same position as his father, waiting for me to die. He sat next to me at the counter in a crowded diner, twiddling his club sandwich and carrying on as if nothing out of the ordinary was occurring. I was lost in thought over my Mother's Day breakfast of steak and eggs, a welcome treat after the strict vegetarian diet I had been on.

The last time I saw Ruth, we were sitting in one of her favorite diners. She looked across the table at me, peering deeply into the windows of my soul, and said, "You have the most beautiful eyes." It was the only time in all the thirteen years I had known Ruth that I felt seen. That morning, I had painstakingly applied make-up because she would often comment, "Honey, you look so much better with lipstick." She never approved of my normal 'a la natural' appearance. But on this day, she didn't even notice the cosmetics that had taken nearly an hour to apply and finally chose instead to look beyond appearances. It was a *mitzvah*, her way of blessing me. I blushed like a young girl receiving a compliment and shifted around in the booth, pulling my dress further down over my legs. Élan and I exchanged a look of astonishment, then warm, sheepish smiles spread over both our faces.

My son and I were preparing Mother's Day dinner when we received Élan's call, telling us that his mom had crossed over. Ruth melted into the black velvet void, unifying with that profound oneness of her spirit. We all come into this world alone, and we all leave it alone. But I prefer to see it as All One, the Holy Spirit, the *Shekinah*.

The spiral of life and death was mirrored in Pyro's abandoned snakeskin, which I found just one hour after Ruth's passing. Placing it in the crystal bowl where I kept all my snakes' sheds, I contemplated how I could make a new beginning out of this ending. Although it was close to midnight, I called my own mother. We discussed her relationship with her mother-in-law, now ninety-four years old. She shared with me the grace with which my grandmother was letting go, singing her swan song of old age and ensuing death. Soon, I would be saying goodbye to Grandma Cleo, too.

I asked my mother how she felt about her own death and what kind of funeral she wanted. She told me that she had already made her own funeral arrangements and that she wanted a Catholic Mass said in her honor. I was relieved to know that I wouldn't have to worry about this detail when her time came.

When we finished our conversation at midnight, long past her bedtime, she said, "Sweetie, I'm glad you called. I love you."

There was an intimacy in our talk that spoke of the bond between a mother and daughter. Time and time again, she had shown me how to grow old with dignity. I walked outside into the black, moonless night, gazed up at the stars, and whispered, "*Shalom*, Ruth, *Shalom*."

I had said my farewells, yes. But I realized that the act of saying goodbye could not, by itself, fully erase the pain inherent in my relationship with Ruth. While meditating one morning, Ammachi—the hugging saint of India—called forth. Two photographs of her sat on my altar. In one, she holds a cobra near her heart, its hood spread as if ready to strike. In another, she dons a coiled cobra like a hat upon her head. The serpent spirals of death and life were guiding me to my next step.

The next month, I traveled to her ashram in Castro Valley, California, where Ammachi was making an annual visit. As I waited in line for my turn—number 539—I clutched the bouquet of orange, lavendar, yellow, and red roses handpicked from someone's carefully tended garden. Like a child, I was bashful and unsure of myself; perhaps neither I, nor the roses, were good enough for this incarnation of Divine Mother.

Ammachi joyously took the bouquet and heartily embraced me. I turned my face away from hers, not feeling worthy enough to be so close to her, but she gently took my head and brought me to her breast. She chanted, "Don Na Ma, Don Na Ma" and kissed me. I returned her kisses with fervor. Enchanted and lulled into a timeless eternity of Mother's divine, radiant love, I wept for joy. My heart came rushing up from beneath the murky surface of resentment like the lotus flower in a pond ready to unfold its petals to the sunlight. In a gush of overwhelming surrender, the hardened sticky places inside me melted like candle wax. My heart was soft and malleable, and in her hands, she could mold it any way she pleased. But Mother simply caught the dripping wax of my emotions in the container of her warm flesh as my tears soaked her white sari.

When it was time to go, it was if I had awoken from a dream of darkness. A song repeated in my head:

> Who tells me thou art dark? Oh, my Mother Divine, Who tells me thou art dark? Oh, my Mother Divine, thousands of suns and moons from thy body do shine, thousands of suns and moons from thy body do shine...

I sailed away with clarity of heart never experienced before.

Mother's come in a multitude of forms. Soaring with Ammachi's love and grounded by the warmth of my biological mother, I could finally let Ruth and all her accompanying baggage go. She could no longer be a prisoner of misery in my psyche. I was restored. I was loved. I was free.

Serpent Spirals of Life and Death

Ammachi with cobra

27

Solstice Snake

The lifeless California King snake lay in the creek bed. Two boys pelted it with rocks. They wanted to smash it even deader than it already was. Their fear had catapulted them into assaulting and cursing the helpless creature.

I was out for my sunset walk with my husband when the boys cavalierly gestured for us to come see their good deed of further crushing the scary, creepy, perceived-as-evil snake. Of course, how could they have known they were barking up the wrong tree?

I immediately insisted that they stop what they were doing and scurried down the embankment to rescue the dead snake from further abuse. Fortunately, they had not killed it. Probably the recent heat waves had baked it to death, or perhaps it had died of starvation. As I bent down to have a closer look, the boys were standing above me on the street shouting, "Oooh, creepy, sick. You're crazy. What are you doing?" Their rock pelting had not damaged the body of the two-foot long, young adult king snake. It lay there with an almost smile on its face, smirking back at the terrified boys. It seemed content to have met its end in the cool, sensuous slime of the creek bed. I blessed it while admiring the repetitive pattern of the black and white bands that encircled its body.

King snakes, unbeknownst to these boys, are the "good" snakes. They are the only creatures known to man or beast that are immune to the venom of the rattlesnake. They are even able to kill rattlesnakes and eat them. They also eat other undesirable vermin and so rightfully earn the title of King Snake. It is never good to kill a King Snake. They are most desirable for keeping the ecological balance of Mother Nature.

I slid a stick underneath the snake's belly and carried Mr. King back up to street level, dangling it from the end of the stick.

As I climbed up, my husband was beaming at me and chuckling under his breath. "These boys don't know who they're dealing with. Sss...snakewoman," he hissed between clenched, bared teeth in a mocking grin.

Meanwhile, the boys were morbidly fascinated, yet still frightened of the limp dead snake. Staying as far away as possible, but as close as they could tolerate, they asked, "What are you going to do with it?"

I said, "I am going to take it home and give it a proper burial."

The boys' fascination got the best of them as they inched in for a closer look.

"This is a California King Snake. See the black and white bands? That's how you can tell it apart from other snakes. These types of snakes are the good guys. There's nothing to be afraid of. It's dead. It won't bite you."

I pointed toward my house, and the boys took off running as though the Loch Ness monster was chasing them. I laughed out loud, flashing back to a funny story from my childhood when my father once frightened all of us that much.

One Halloween, Dad—dressed up like a cannibal—scared not only all the neighborhood kids, but all the moms, too. He tied a grass skirt around his waist and put on a funky black wig. He blobbed black paint all over his body and smeared himself with dried fish, the kind the Japanese use for making soup broth. He stunk to high heaven. To top it off, he carried a black plastic severed pygmy head in one hand and a frog gig in his other hand. A frog gig is a long, wooden stick with a sharp metal trident at the end, used for spearing the frogs that Dad would bring home for a Southern-style fried frog legs dinner.

I remember how it would give us kids the creeps when he was cleaning them. He would shake salt over those frog legs and they would twitch and jump as though they were still alive. We thought they would jump right out of the frying pan and chase us down the street. We loved the taste of those fried frog legs, though. They had a delicious flavor more delicate and juicy than fried chicken.

But that year, no one in the neighborhood got candy at our house because everyone ran away in terror of my father's trick before they could get their treat. My siblings and I were delighted; we got to eat all the leftover candy. Kids and their moms would come to the door, take one look at Dad, who let out a big grunt while raising the frog gig up, and off they would go. I never saw my father laugh so hard in all his life when one "Leave It to Beaver" type mom with pumps on her feet like Mrs. Cleaver, fell over backwards, her legs sprawled in the air, tangled in her 50's dress before she was able to get up and run away. My father was definitely king of the pranksters in his costume as the proverbial headhunting cannibal.

As I watched those boys shoot down the street as fast as an arrow, headed straight for the target, I enjoyed the sheer glee that Dad must have felt that Halloween.

"Stop, slow down. That's my house," I hollered at them. "Come on in and see some live snakes. Don't worry, they're in cages."

By the time I caught up with them, I had already given them all the available admonitions in my arsenal about why California King snakes were good for the environment.

"These boys are getting a real biology lesson from Mother 'Snakewoman' Nature herself," my husband said.

I chased those boys right into my house with that poor pathetic dead snake on the end of the stick. While they peered into the cages of my four snakes, I gave them an education on non-poisonous snakes. They looked into the glass aquarium cages at my two adult Ball Pythons, the baby Corn snake, and the young Red-tailed Columbian Boa. They commented, "Boy, I'm glad they're in cages. Don't let 'em out. Okay?"

I took the dead snake into my back yard and placed it near a statue of a serpent. This is a favorite spot in my garden where I often do yoga and make prayers and offerings. I carefully coiled the snake in a spiral on the soft green baby's tears planted there. They still wanted to know what I was going to do with it. Remembering the fiasco with Green Leaf, I thought here was my second chance. I told them I wanted the ants to pick the bones clean, so I could make a necklace out of it. They both let out a grossed-out moan.

I went into the garage to find a screen to place over it, but couldn't find anything but a second-hand lady's tennis racket stashed in a cobweb-filled corner. I reached up, grabbed it, and brought it out to the yard, sneering at my husband that this useless piece of junk he bought years ago at a garage sale in hopes that he would take up tennis again was actually a Lady Slazenger woman's racket but would finally be put to good use anyway. The boys wanted to know if we played badminton. I said, "No, I'm going to use this as a screen to hold the snake down while it decomposes and the critters eat its flesh, so no other animal can get it." I placed it over the snake and put two very large rocks on either side to secure it.

By this time, Liam was teaching them how to shoot arrows with his bow. He set up his target on the hay bales that we had stacked up for his archery practice, and soon all three boys were enjoying a new focus as mock Robin Hoods. Élan stayed out in the yard, giving them tips and making sure they didn't shoot each other.

The next morning was Father's Day. I walked out into the garden to look at the King under the tennis racket, but there was no sign of it. He was gone, vanished. I wondered if it had come back to life and slithered away. More likely, some hungry animal, a raccoon maybe, had a gourmet dinner last night. Oh well, I still didn't get my snake bone necklace. I mused upon the adventures of the Summer Solstice Snake—here yesterday, gone today. The sun was turning from its zenith of light in the summer toward the darkness of winter. I smiled a snaky smile and gave thanks to the teachings from the natural world. The Suburban Snake Priestess struck again, teaching the children something about the stark realities of life and death through the serpent.

28

Minoan Snake Priestess

The snake was known as the vehicle of immortality. In ancient times a gigantic snake was thought to wind over the whole universe, stretched around the "universal egg." The snake was the guardian and evoker of spontaneous life energy and vitality, the energy of growing plants, animals, and pregnancy. In Greek mythology, the Snake Goddess shares the realms of the earth, water, the underworld. She rules the heavenly waters, and her fearsome expression is a reminder of volcanic eruptions, tidal waves, and earthquakes that have and will continue to cause destruction. The sacred snakes entwined around her wrists offer life or death and represent the rebirth of all life. She wears a crown of roses and a small leopard sits on her head. She is a Goddess of primal energy, life, death, and regeneration, trance, shedding fear, and renewing hope. She was the head Goddess of the ancient Minoans in the Mediterranean. They lived in peace for over 1000 years.

—Soaring Eagle

THE DREAM OF THE SNAKE PRIESTESS

The water and the customs and the white mud
are beneath me far below
I stand high on a mountain top
I have climbed here at dusk
In my bare priestess feet
Have walked up the rocky crested butte
To take my stance
My snakes have guided the way
through infra-red/feeling vision
Though I stood *in the blind water*
My two snakes have uncoiled
Have risen to bite me again and again
        Ida Nadi
        Pingala Nadi
I breathe the twin serpents up my shushumna channel
The core of my body
My spine
Reverberates with copper and gold
Glows the sun itself setting
Gleaming inside me
Poised in my seven-chakra tiered skirt
Bare-breasted heart
Leopard on my head crowned with roses
I stand
Offering my two snakes
to the sky
The flutter of Seraphim
Winged angelic serpents
Come
And I am lifted up
By the *light, the pressure of nameless fingertips*
Carry me into the no moon night
Where I meet my starry sisters
The Pleiades
At the head of the Medusa
Where all the veils are lifted
And we circle
In the Spiral of the Serpent

                                            —Le'ema

Lines in italics are taken from Pablo Neruda's The Ruined Street *translated by Robert Bly.*

Minoan Snake Priestess

Often people who have seen my dances are surprised at how small I am when they meet me in person. They say I appear bigger on-stage. The Minoan Snake Priestess affects me in a similar way. I am drawn to her more than any other Goddess statue. Perhaps it is because she feels so large energetically despite her diminutive physicality. At just thirteen inches tall, she has grandeur, wild beauty, and passionate self-expression. The wide-eyed, entranced look on her face touches me in a place where I feel most awakened. Even as a young child, I loved being in that state of wonder, listening to the voices of the invisible realms, so far yet so near. It was more real to me than so-called reality, and often I was surprised at the accuracy of my vision.

I imagine her being alert and alive at a time when she would have been revered for her prophetic gifts rather than reviled. Perhaps her expression is a reflection of seeing the volcanic eruptions, tidal waves, and earthquakes that probably ended the high Minoan civilization. Her bare breasts and open chest show a heart full of love, compassion, and wisdom, but also a fully embodied sexuality that energizes us with a mere glance. This Goddess from Crete radiates *Shakti*. For me, she is as awesome as the mystery of life itself.

Yet, the Minoan Snake Priestess seems to defy description by even the most adept scholars. Archaeologist Sir Arthur Evans first identified certain Minoan artifacts as Snake Goddesses in 1903 CE. The most famous was found in a shrine underneath the temple-palace of Knossos, dating from about 1600 BCE. The function of the Minoan Serpent figurines is unknown. Some believe they were used in ritual to influence the Goddess to proffer favorable conditions.

All Snake Goddess figurines found in Crete have two elements in common: the flounced skirt and the snakes. The one I admire the most has outstretched arms with two poisonous adders clasped in her hands. She looks as though she is holding lightning bolts. This figurine's face magnifies the moment of spiritual insight when the mortal priestess metamorphoses into the Living Goddess.

For many years, I yearned to dance the Minoan Snake Goddess with my two pythons, but I never felt worthy of the privilege. My critical scholar self warned that I wasn't knowledgeable enough to accept the honor. Who was I to portray such an icon?

But one afternoon, Dhyanis announced that the summer Goddess Show would be called *Atlantia*. She asked if I would perform the Cretan Snake Goddess dance and even offered to help me design the costume. By now the millennium had arrived, and humankind hadn't been destroyed by an apocalyptic catastrophe as some had predicted. What's more, it was the Year of the Dragon. *My* year. The timing felt magical. It was a serendipitous offer, and I couldn't refuse.

The bell-shaped skirt of the Snake Goddess is a sacred garment, enhancing the female power. The symbols on the skirt represent her energy, and the apron covering the pubic area focuses that power. The skirt is so commanding that I felt a special ritual was required to make it.

Luck was on my side when I entered a fabric store and found an array of cloth from around the world. Satins, brocades, velvets of various colors, and textures spun me into an exotic world separate from the one outside. The necessary material for constructing the garment of my revered Snake Goddess seemed to find me. Translucent silks woven with golden threads in all the colors of the rainbow lay on a table in the center of the store.

As I lingered, absorbed in this luscious fabric that smelled of Indian incense, the vision of the costume revealed itself to me. The skirt would have seven layers, each a different color to represent the seven chakras. The bottom tier would be green for the earth and the heart of the Goddess, and then move up through blue, purple, red, and orange, reaching a band of yellow around the waist that represented the Goddess' power. It took a while to calculate the amount needed for each piece since it had to be doubled to create the ruffled flounce of the skirt. The black tulle apron would have gold trim forming crosshatched diamond patterns. The top would be copper-colored silk with black trim around the sleeves and upper waist to accentuate my bare breasts.

As for the feline on her crowning headpiece, well, I shall never unriddle the cat. What breed was it? And how did it come to stand serenely at the top of her skull?

I wanted to personify the statue of the Minoan Snake Goddess—to show how such an artifact might come to life. At first, I imagined I could dance with my own kitty standing on my head but soon realized the sheer folly of this wish. No cat would stay on anyone's head for even a minute, let alone through a whole dance with live snakes. And besides, this isn't a circus act, I reasoned.

Immediately after purchasing the fabric for the costume, I cruised over to Open Secret Bookstore where the perfect music made itself available. When I walked through the door, it was waiting for me, perched on the display counter in front. Allesandra Belloni's newly-released CD, *Tarantala: Dance of the Ancient Spider*, caught my eye. I picked it up knowing instantly the right song for the dance was on it. Then I sped home and sat on the floor with the fabric strewn around me, listened intently to the CD and lost myself in an ancient future about to be conceived.

But back to that cat...I pulled out my goddess books, searching for a clue to this fabulous feline's mounted glory. Some scholars surmise that the Minoan Snake Goddess may have been erroneously reconstructed with one of the small faience animals, a cat, also found in an area of the excavation of Knossos called the Triple Shrine. This did not deter me, however, for I knew that the lion and the leopard are both associated with the Goddess in many cultures. Traditionally, they were seen as the guardians. Layne Redmond says, "They guard the gate that separates the sacred from the profane, the sanctuary from the outer world, the living from the dead." The cat, coupled with the snakes on the figurine, seemed to depict her as a Goddess of sexuality or fertility. And with the exposure of her full, rounded breasts, her sexual attributes were further emphasized, perhaps indicating that She was a Mother Goddess. More research revealed that the cat and the snakes together may have symbolized the afterlife.

With all this information buzzing inside my brain, I decided to wear a stuffed leopard on top of my head. Yet again, the perfect solution presented itself when I entered a store called Animal Kingdom. There, in the window, was the cutest leopard, in the exact size I needed for my crown. It looked almost real. The man behind the register looked at me quizzically when I held the cat up to my head and asked for a mirror, but I didn't care. I'm on a mission, I told myself, and nothing will deter me from getting the costume I need to dance this Goddess.

The next day, I took the fabric to Dhyanis. We put our hands on the material and blessed it, asking the Goddess to energize our work. I had just recently been with Ammachi, where I received a mantra, so I chanted that secret word under my breath through the entire process of making the costume. The sound vibration filled every cut, every stitch, and every action of sewing.

For hours and hours we worked to create the wondrous garment of the Minoan Snake Goddess. One by one, I gathered all seven of the flounces, spacing the ruffles with my fingers. Dhyanis sewed them onto the bell-shaped underskirt made from sheer white organza.

Over the years, Dhyanis has made many costumes for me. She has the hands of a magician and always seems to bring forth the costumes of my visions. But this was the best one yet! After three days, we completed our labor of love. When I tried the garment on for the final fitting, we burst into tears and laughed delightedly at our accomplishment. I knew that when I wore it, I would appear as the Goddess.

Dhyanis exclaimed, "You got the prize this year. I can't wait to see the dance!"

On the evening of the performance, Dyhanis ushered me into a private dressing room. Backstage, I was more nervous than usual as I warmed up while listening to the music with headphones from a portable CD player. I prayed for the creative force to pour through me and revitalize the lives of the community. I prayed for the ability to imbue the divine into the spatial configurations of the dance. And I prayed to be of service in my power.

∼

The dance begins in the dark. I stand upstage with my back to the audience, facing the hand-painted silk backdrop of a palace temple on a hillside under a full moon mirrored upon the sparkling blue Aegean Sea. Stately and upright, poised and potent, full of raw electric energy, I can barely move—a chthonian portrayal as the Minoan Snake Goddess. I hold the snakes in my hands; their lithe bodies entwine around my arms, which cross over my breasts. A mandolin accompanies the vocal overtone chanting of the singer in a plaintive introduction. My body sways and then spirals counter-clockwise while my feet are planted firmly in place. Slowly, I turn my face to the audience, one side and then the other, with a soulful expression. Then I turn my body around—the statue coming to life. I circle forward in precise steps, returning to the present day—an ancient priestess in ceremonial posture in a formal rite.

There, in the very center, my breasts are revealed as I lower my arms down, out, around, ultimately rising into the Minoan Snake Goddess's provocative stance. I hold this posture for one full measure and then walk on the tips of my toes downstage, the snakes held high in the air. When I reach the edge of the stage, I lift the snakes to my third eye. Their forked tongues lick my face and ears as though whispering primeval secrets to me. My hypnotic state deepens. I lower the snakes to my breasts, and holding them like suckling infants, I rock them in my arms and sway from side to side.

The serpent energy stimulates me, and I begin to glide in the infinity symbol, holding one snake high and one low, alternating sides. A series of grapevine steps leads me into a spinning crescendo; my face looks toward the heavens, the snakes outstretched from my hands. The flounces on the skirt create a whirling matrix of the chakras, and I become the embodiment of our double helix DNA. I am wide open, a vessel exuding love, blessing all who witness.

∼

As I made my way off stage, I was overcome with emotion. *Oh my, what have I done? What hath the Goddess wrought?* In the beginning, I felt shy and vulnerable, wary to expose myself as a vessel for the spirit of the Goddess. But in the costume, we merged, and I grew to fit her. Transported, I forgot myself. My attunement was so complete that I stood transfixed, staring at myself in the dressing room mirror with honeyed eyes of mystic wisdom. A larger-than-life energy swirled around my body and shimmered in my aura.

It took awhile to get back into present time. Once my snakes were put back into their basket, I removed the headdress, slipped out of the magical garment, and looked at my naked body with wonder and gratitude. A prayer came to my lips. "Thank you, dear Goddess, for allowing me to be the vehicle for Your radiant presence, for guiding and keeping me on this path of Your sacred dance. This four chambered mansion in my chest will forever be Your dwelling place."

Le'ema as the Minoan Snake Priestess

29

Rosary Snake

Autumn time, red leaves fall
While the weeping sky looks over all
Demeter sadly walks the land
The dying grasses in Her hand...

My heart caught fire at the sight of the orange-red pyracantha bush bursting forth on the walking trail. Tears welled up behind my eyes as I picked a cluster of berries off the bush and held them to my breast. Waves of gratitude and sorrow simultaneously washed over me. I clung to the bright berries while tears splashed down my face like a sudden rainstorm.

My beloved grandmother had died recently. Grandma Cleo loved to decorate her home for Thanksgiving and Christmas with cuttings of pyracantha berries. She was speaking to me from the other side through Mother Nature. I could hear her: "Pyracantha has always been one of my favorite plants. It is a hardy evergreen shrub that blooms in the fall. See how it grows in the full sun, absorbing the sun's fire. That's why they call it pyracantha. See its oval-shaped, little leaves, and its spindly branches with thorns. See how it produces these draping, grape-like clusters of bright and happy berries that the birds love to eat but are inedible for humans. I will always be near you at this time of year in the pyracanthas. Whenever you pick a sprig, I'll be here, right next to your heart as I am now." So I picked a sprig of pyracantha to adorn my kitchen table. At home, I placed them in a vase next to a gold candle in her honor.

It was just before Halloween—season for the ancestors, when the veil between the worlds is thin—mere days after Grandma's funeral, when I stumbled upon this fiery bush on my walk through the Marin Hills. I had seen it growing in neighborhoods around homes but never in the wild amidst bay laurel and oak trees. As I held the berries to my heart, they spoke to me of my grandmother's courageous life. They spoke of the mysteries that can only be understood between two souls, between two women, a grandmother and a granddaughter. The mysteries of wild things that grow berries and thorns and are ever-green, the mysteries of a woman's wildish nature, of her instinctual self, of her heart, of her rhythmic cycles, and of her spiritual longings.

There will be no pyracantha berries in Grandma's home this Christmas. She has taken her rightful place in the unknown heavenly wilds, somewhere in the sacred grove between the oak trees and the bay laurels. I will have to celebrate with her in nature this year, a farewell for all her years of wisdom.

As a little girl, I believed that Grandma Cleo was named after Cleopatra. She was the most mysterious and exotic woman I had ever known. She had dark brown hair and gentle warm brown eyes. She always dressed elegantly adding that extra special something to her outfit by her choice of costume jewelry. My favorite piece was her charm bracelet. She would tell me stories of the places she had visited around the world, represented by a trinket on the chain around her wrist. A miniature Arc de Triomphe and the Eiffel Tower cast in pewter kept memories alive of a time when she lived and traveled in Europe with her husband, my step-grandfather, who was in the Air Force. To hear her talk, it must have been one of the happiest times in her life.

She had raised two sons by herself during the Great Depression, a time when the term "single parenthood" was unknown. Her first husband, my grandfather, had left her for another woman without ever saying goodbye. To feed her children, she went to work without having an education or training of any kind. She forged ahead courageously, though it must have broken her heart.

Bright, happy, and cheerful most of time, Grandma Cleo was like those pyracantha berries, full of warmth and sunshine, with a smile like a Cheshire cat and an infectious laugh. She loved telling colorful tales of the places she had been. "I didn't like Amarillo, Texas at all. It was too hot, dry and dusty, and its twisters and tornadoes scared me to death. Sacramento, California was the heart of the Gold Rush Country, but its rainy winters did not suit my temperament. Hawaii was lush with its sweet tropical flowers and beautiful birds, but it still wasn't home." She seemed to prefer living in El Paso, Texas, near the banks of the Rio Grande River, though I imagined she would have been just as happy in Germany on the Rhine.

To my child's eyes, she surely must have descended from some lineage of the Great Goddess. Clio is one of the Nine Muses from the classical Greek period. She is the Goddess of history and is associated with the trumpet. Surely, if Grandma Cleo was not named after Cleopatra, then she must have been named after one of the muses. My priestess eyes would see it no other way. And as her granddaughter, I have been entranced by the muse of dance, Terpsichore. Like the muse, my Grandma Cleo has been a goddess of inspiration for me.

I flew to Texas for her funeral just days after the exhilaration of leading my Snake Priestess retreat for twenty women. What a shock! Jumping on a plane for a funeral was almost more than my body could bear. My spirits were high, however, so I asked if I could facilitate her funeral since I was a legal minister. It would have been pushing the envelope too much for some to have the eldest grandchild, who left Texas and never returned, who had gone from being a nice Catholic girl to a belly dancing priestess, say a funeral, so the answer was no. I was polite and decided to patiently await my opportunity for words at some other time.

In her final years, Grandma Cleo devoted much of her time to praying the Rosary. Ruby red rosary beads, the garland of the Goddess, graced her bony fingers like a luminous snake as she lay resting in her casket. The Deacon had come every Monday morning to pray with her and they became good friends.

At her rosary service, the night before the funeral, I rushed up to the Deacon to ask for a spare rosary. He didn't have one but instead handed me a metal circle with a red crucifix extending from it. It had ten bead-like protrusions around the circle for saying the Hail Marys on. Oh, sweet Jesus, I was in bliss. This was an ankh, the Egyptian symbol of eternal life carried by the Goddess Isis. Isis/Mother Mary, Horus/Jesus. I went deeply into the inner sanctum of my temple space. I was a priestess come to a sacred ceremony of the after-life.

The rosary series with all its Hail Mary's incorporates the Joyful mysteries, the Luminous mysteries, the Sorrowful mysteries, and the Glorious mysteries. It is still my favorite prayer practice and has been the most powerful prayer for me in times of great need and even danger. It saved me once from being raped. By repeating it out loud, my assailant stopped his assault and left me alone. Divine Mother is truly a protector of her children. That is why she is often called our intercessor. She intercedes on our behalf if we are open for her guidance.

The manner in which the Deacon delivered these prayers was imbued with the power of Divine Mother's mystery and absolutely 'Full of Grace.' Behind him on the wall was a tapestry of The Virgin of Guadalupe who seemed to be giving him the inspiration that sparked his noble recitation of the rosary. When he finished, the Deacon asked if anyone wanted to say something about Grandma Cleo. This was my chance.

When I stood up to speak, a surge of grace and dignity pulsed through me. "My grandmother, or Grandma Cleo as she became affectionately known by all who knew her, including her own children, was a lover of life. In spite of all her hardships, she embraced life to its fullest. She loved roses and Rembrandt. Her favorite perfume was Jean Pateau. She was still on a first name basis, at age ninety-something, with the salesgirl at the cosmetics counter at Macy's where she purchased her Esteé Lauder anti-aging cream. When I was a child spending the night at Grandma's house, I loved watching her put that cream on her face through the reflection in the round mirror of her art deco dresser. She had flawless skin until the day she died. She was a living beauty in the truest sense…"

Grandma broke her collarbone and hipbone when she fell after pulling herself free from the restraining straps in her bed in the nursing home. She seemed to be orchestrating her own death, enduring the medical interference of major surgery only to survive for a few days. During that time, when anyone asked her how she was doing, she would smile and say, "Fine." She knew her time was at hand, and she was at peace. She was a brave soul, as attested to by the little plaque that hung in her dining room with a quote from Bette Davis: "Old age is not for sissies." I feel so lucky to have had this woman in my life for forty-eight years out of her ninety-three.

On the flight home to California, I sat next to a beautiful woman, a born again Christian who quoted the Bible to me. We had a discussion about religion. I was shy at first to tell her I worshipped the Mother of God, Divine Mother, but eventually I did. She then pronounced that because my prayers weren't addressed to Jesus, they weren't being heard. Whoa! At that moment, I felt a gush of blood spurt out between my legs and spill onto the airplane seat through my thin skirt. Somehow, I stayed in the conversation, becoming bold enough to tell her that Mary Magdalene was not the prostitute she was made out to be and that she was the bride of Christ when I felt another spurt of blood spill forth. I quickly grabbed the jeans I had been holding and rushed back to the tiny airplane john to change. Bright red blood was everywhere—all over my skirt, underwear, jeans, and now even my hands.

I felt an odd kind of prideful shame as I came back to my seat. There was a big spot where I had been sitting, and more than likely this woman had seen my accident. Fortunately, the airline blankets were a maroon color so I took one in hopes that it would cover the bloodstain. I felt like the Scarlet Whore herself, but the priestess within me knew that on some level, I was consecrating that plane as sacred space, just as Jesus consecrated the wine as his blood in the communion cup, originally the menstrual blood of the Goddess.

The Sacred Heart of Mary, pierced with thorns but crowned with roses, broken yet open. The berries, the berries, the blood red berries of the Goddess—the Black Madonna, the Guadalupe, the Magdalene. My Grandmother loved the color red—rose red, raspberry red, apple red, pomegranate red, poppy red, pyracantha red.

On a mystical level, I am sure that my Grandmother understood the red of blood. Blood of life, blood of death, her blood no longer red, her blood still.

As the plane descended, I looked down at my fingernails, painted the color of a crimson desert, and contemplated phrases from the poem, "Thunder, Perfect Mind," from the *Nag Hammadi* texts:

For I am the first and the last.
I am the honored one and the scorned one.
I am the whore and the holy one.
I am the wife and the virgin.
I am the mother and the daughter....

I am knowledge and ignorance.
I am shame and boldness.
I am shameless; I am ashamed.
I am strength and I am fear.
I am war and peace.
Give heed to me.
I am the one who is disgraced and the great one.

30

Snake Sage

With hands on her hips, the mom glared down at me. "You don't actually believe in all this shit, do you?"

I looked up at her from my seat at the Egyptian Banquet. My hand froze, fork poised in mid-air.

Her behavior cast a shadow over what had been a glorious event for the fifth grade class at the Waldorf School. The children were studying the civilization of Ancient Egypt. As part of their learning in a Waldorf curriculum, they were offered an experience through dance and ritual theater that embodied the energies of what Ancient Egypt might have looked and felt like. Because I am an ordained priestess of Isis with experience leading rituals and performing sacred dances, I was asked to facilitate this special evening.

But in all my years of performing sacred dance and leading rituals, I had never received a comment like this one. I stood up. My feet moved deep into the earth, grounding my energy. An opening of patient, calm energy pulsed up through the soles of my feet, through my legs and hips, centering itself in my belly. An unexpected, effortless flow of grace showered down from the crown of my head, pouring into the center of my heart. I felt the love of the Goddess move compassionately toward the upset woman.

"I am a priestess of Isis," I said.

Holding my ground seemed to disturb her more. She grabbed her boy and huffed off, yelling out to the other parents, "No son of mine is going to play with the son of a witch!"

With the teacher's encouragement, I had taught the children ancient Pharoahnic movements that illustrated the story of the Ma'at, Goddess of Divine Justice in the Egyptian pantheon. According to Egyptian beliefs, it is she whom we meet after we die. Her age-old story explores the soul's journey after death. In the Osirian Hall of Judgment, the departed's heart is laid on one side of her scales. On the other side, she places an ostrich plume, plucked from her headdress. If the heart is heavier than her feather, it is tossed to the bloodthirsty, hippopotamus-lion-crocodile monster named Ammit. But if the heart is equal or lighter than her feather, Ma'at, in the form of the winged-Isis, embraces us and we go a happy afterlife. The children did a marvelous job re-enacting her story through dance.

Many of the parents, determined to make this event a memorable one, also created ritual enactments for the children as if they were going through an ancient mystery school. In small groups, the children were led through tests of the four elements of earth, air, fire, and water.

The children didn't know what would transpire, but they prepared themselves as neophytes ready to undergo initiation by fasting on liquids all day. They were also instructed to rest in the afternoon and bathe by candlelight. When they arrived at school, they put on white vestments. Parents painted Egyptian eyes on each of them using kohl eyeliner.

Donning a black wig with tiny braids decorated with golden beads, I greeted the children as the Goddess Isis. I wore gowns and robes of rich purples, golds, and silvers for the sequence of events that would come.

It was a cold January evening. The rains pelted down as we gathered under a porch to begin the ritual. Some of the parents exchanged concerned looks.

A grandmother next to me grabbed my arm. "The children can't traipse through the rain all night. They'll get sick!"

I stood by as the seasoned Waldorf teacher and parents nodded their heads in agreement that we would continue. This was an initiation, after all. The rain only added to the atmosphere.

I spoke loudly to the excited children. "Here is a chant to invoke the lion-headed Goddess, Sekhmet, to guide and protect you on your journey through the four elements...*Sa Sekem Sahu, Sa Sekem Sahu, Sa Sekem Sahu*...She will give you courage and strength to face these tests. Now, go forth with blessings."

At that instant, a bolt of lightning blasted from the sky, striking the ground a few feet from where I stood. The children shot up into the air, screeching with fright.

"You may proceed," I told them, my voice calm despite my racing heartbeat.

As soon as we stepped out into the night, the rain ceased. It was as if that lightning bolt was the exclamation point that announced, "Go for it!"

For the element of Earth, Élan dressed as Thoth, the Ibis-headed scribe and teacher God. He wore a full-length white robe, a headdress shaped like an Ibis with a long beak, and an Egyptian cloth around his neck and shoulders. He and the children built a pyramid out of copper piping. They learned how to measure the dimensions based upon the circumference of a circle using only a stick and a string. The end result was a six-foot pyramid, perfectly proportioned to the measurements of the Great Pyramid of Giza. It was a hands-on geometry lesson!

For the element of air, a parent blindfolded the children and guided them to the school playground, where they climbed up a rope ladder to the top platform and removed their blindfolds. Standing beneath an overcast sky, they inhaled the moist night air into their lungs and recited a chant about air, our sacred breath.

They were then led to the test for water. A parent had placed a blue tarp inside the sandbox and filled it with water and dry ice. One by one, the children crossed the bubbling, smoking water on a balance beam.

Last, the children were tested through fire. Another parent had created an exquisite altar inside the Eurythmy Room, bright with candles and candelabra. The neophytes were asked to light four candles amongst hundreds of lit candles. Afterwards, they had to find the ones they selected and extinguish them with a candle snuff.

With the tests complete, the children performed their story of Ma'at. I followed with a dance called *Isis of the Snakes,* a refined and elegant piece illustrating through arm gestures and hand *mudras* the rising energy of serpent power, the *Kundalini.*

I removed my robe to reveal a purple and lapis lazuli-colored beaded evening gown from the 1940s, purchased at an antique store eons ago when I fancied I might become a movie star. The dress had served for the past twenty years in the role of my Isis costume, the first piece I had choreographed in my repertoire of *Healing Goddess* dances. In those days, I wasn't dancing with snakes, but the serpentine energy guided me nonetheless.

I gathered my snakes from their basket backstage, placing one around each arm and cradling their heads in my hands. They centered themselves between my wrists and the crook in my elbow, looking very archetypal, and lifted their heads to my face.

The parents had never seen me dance, let alone in a sultry evening gown with my snakes. The suspense rose in the room as I prepared for my entrance. The dance is only a three-minute piece, but it carries a quality of eternity that is palpable. The room was silent as I spun to my left, dervish-style, with the snakes draped over my arms. When the piece ended, I bowed with my arms and snakes crossed over my heart.

Before I could finish asking if anyone wanted to hold my snakes, the hand of every child popped up. The parents seemed astonished at their children's enthusiasm. One parent, a red-headed beauty named Kerry, was shocked that her daughter liked snakes. But I wasn't surprised. The previous year, I had brought my snakes into the classroom, and all the children loved them. I received many color pencil drawings as a thank you. Several of these delightful works of art are now in my Sacred Serpent Slide Show.

For the final ritual of the evening, I stood as the Goddess Isis inside the grand pyramid. It shimmered in the candlelight, giving off a mysterious glow. The children were called up individually to enter the pyramid. They placed scrolls, inscribed with their intentions for the coming year, into a basket on the altar. I anointed them on the forehead with special oil blended from Cinnamon, Frankincense, Rose, Jasmine, and Lotus—sacred herbs and flowers to the Ancient Egyptians. It is said these essential oils bring protection, health, happiness, and love. All of the children were earnest and open in offering their scrolls and receiving Isis's blessing. Their souls were yearning to be seen—to be touched by the divine! Looking into their eyes, I placed a bronze ankh amulet, a symbol of eternal life, around their necks and whispered, "You are a child of the Goddess Isis. I bless you now and for all eternity." It was an honor to be of service in awakening them to their unique essence as a child of Divine Mother.

At the elegant but simple Egyptian banquet, several parents congratulated me on coordinating the project.

"You master-minded a fabulous event," Élan told me.

Glowing with pride, I said, "I couldn't have done it without the Goddess, the teachers, and the parents."

We proceeded to indulge ourselves. The food was set on a gold-brocade tablecloth upon golden platters. The children, ravenous from their adventure, devoured the stuffed grape leaves, cucumber salad, tabouli and hummus, pita bread, and a Moroccan couscous.

It was at that moment that the woman bellowed out her insult. The energy in the room switched from celebration and expansion to contraction. I watched in horror as she grabbed her son and stormed out of the room. The scene felt frozen in time as if someone had hit a pause button.

When we recovered enough to resume the celebration, a reserved air remained. Not a word was said about the incident, but the hushed atmosphere disturbed me. I felt shamed and misunderstood but did my best to brush it off. After all, it was not my responsibility to deal with this woman. I was just a volunteer parent doing exactly what I had been asked to do.

The next day, the woman's son did not return to the classroom—or the day after, or the day after that. She removed him from the school on the assumption that it was practicing what she perceived to be religion. She accused the school of being a cult, even claiming that the selections from classical literature the children had recited were a form of brainwashing.

A few days later, I got a call from another Waldorf mom. "Le'ema I want to thank you for the powerful experience! As soon as I'm off the phone, I'm going to write a letter to the board and tell them how lucky we are to have you as a mom in our school," she said, adding, "When that idiot woman came up to me, I told her I was a priestess, too. But I have a different tradition. I'm a Wiccan priestess."

Now I understood why I had been called a witch. When we hung up, I figured this would be the end of it.

A month later, I attended a classroom meeting at a parent's home. Kerry showed me into the living room. A fire crackled in the fireplace and candles burned in the corners of the room. A lovely array of food was set upon the dining room table. Everything looked cozy enough, but something felt wrong. I couldn't help but notice there were more parents at this meeting than usual.

Kerry started by introducing one of the board members who would discuss the hiring of next year's teacher. I began to relax. But after the board member spoke, the tension still hung about like a black cloud ready to let loose a thunderstorm. Inevitably, it arrived.

Kerry's ex-husband, a lawyer named Roger, demanded to know what had happened at the Egyptian event. "Were you practicing black magic on my child?" he asked indignantly.

Since the man rarely attended school events, much less classroom meetings, the parents in the room were collectively stunned by his aggressive stance. Roger was an estate attorney, but he was acting like a puffed-up prosecuting criminal lawyer.

Kerry slumped down into her chair, looking as if she wanted to hide from the ensuing onslaught.

To ease the strain, one of the parents jokingly remarked, "Yeah, Le'ema, tell us all about paganism and witchcraft."

Roger continued to pelt me with questions and accusations. I sat on the edge of the chair, my feet in moccasins planted on the floor. I shook my head from side to side, both to say no and as a reflex to clear my energy field. The turquoise and silver feather earrings from New Mexico jingled against my cheeks.

Summoning courage, I spoke, "I am a Priestess of Isis, and I am a sacred dancer. I did what the teacher and the parents asked of me. I did nothing to harm the children."

"I've been getting phone calls from this mother who says you're practicing witchcraft and brainwashing our children," he went on.

"I'm not brainwashing them," I replied. "I'm devoted to the Divine Feminine. I showed the children how one can embody the qualities of beauty, dignity, and nobility."

Kerry piped in. "She works with the Goddess energy, Roger. I would think you would appreciate having your daughters see the beautiful gifts she brings. Le'ema is—"

Her inflamed ex-husband cut her off. "Are you or are you not a witch?"

"What is this, a trial for witch-burning? Are we in Salem?" Kerry demanded. "Come on, Roger, get a life. Le'ema did something of great beauty that moved all of us. She's not a witch. And besides, you weren't even there."

The standoff was mounting between them. A couple of women looked at each other as if to say, "No wonder she divorced this guy."

A dad in the back of the room spoke up. "The Waldorf approach to education has always stressed the importance of experiential learning for children. Many of the main lessons are accompanied by a cultural event to give the children the flavor of a time and place in history. It gives them a context, rather than just a concept. We wanted our children to experience the Egyptian mysteries through a theatrical event."

Roger didn't respond. The teacher took advantage of the respite to wrap up housekeeping details. When she finished, Roger rushed out the door.

Kerry approached me. "I'm so sorry, Le'ema. Roger can be such a jerk."

"Don't worry about it," I told her. "This is the Year of the Serpent. It's time to shed some old patriarchal skins."

This was true: yet again, we had to shed the worn out ways of being. Even so, I couldn't help but wish that the journey of the Divine Feminine didn't have to be such an arduous climb.

When I got home, my calm exterior vanished, and I fell into a heap on the floor.

"It's just one woman," Élan said, trying in vain to comfort me.

"But now the whole school thinks I'm a witch! I'm not a witch. I don't cast spells. I am a priestess."

At that moment, one of my deities hanging on the wall, the Black Madonna, crashed to the floor. Élan and I watched in disbelief. This freaked me out even more. I couldn't sleep that night.

The next morning I phoned my mentor, Nicki Scully, and spilled out the whole story.

"Tell me what to do," I cried, "I'm so scared!"

"Le'ema listen," she comforted. "Take a deep breath. Now, you're not scared. You're just dyslexic. Turn the "c" and the "a" around in that word."

At first, I didn't get it. My brow knit, then a shy smile spread across my face like a little girl who had just solved a riddle. "You mean I'm not scared, I'm s-a-c-r-e-d."

"Yes, exactly! You are sacred. If someone had a powerful experience in your presence, this means that you did your work. You should be proud of yourself."

Nicki told me that my deity falling was an omen of protection, that the Divine Mother took the hit of this negative energy toward me.

Four months later, on a warm June afternoon, the class presented a play on the Greek mysteries in the outdoor amphitheatre. While the parents waited for the performance to begin, Kerry and her daughter wandered off into the fields beyond the playground. They returned, together carrying a large, golden snake with coppery brown spots. They presented him to me.

"What kind of snake is this?" the eight-year-old asked me, wide-eyed with wonder while curling her finger around his tail.

Of all the invisible gifts I had ever received, this was one of the best. I had taught them to honor the snake, to respond with love not fear.

"I think he's a gopher snake. They're harmless and good for the environment. They eat the gophers that destroy the roots of plants in the garden, making those holes we sprain our ankles in. They come out in the sun to warm themselves during the day so they can hunt at night. Go release him where you found him so he can do his job."

The mother/daughter duo, a modern day Demeter and Persephone, turned and happily sauntered into the late afternoon sun, their red hair glimmering like halos around them.

Content that my work had made a contribution, I let out a long "SSS" sigh of relief.

31

Athena ~ Greek Serpent Goddess

Red lipstick, purple eye shadow, pink cheek-blush, and black eyeliner extended out to make snake eyes—this was my make-up meditation, transforming me into tonight's goddess dancer. First would come Quan Yin, riding in on the tail of the dragon in the Year of the Serpent, followed by Isis of the Snakes, the Serpent in the Garden, Lamia, Medusa, Athena, and the Minoan Snake Goddess. How I loved the beauty of my backstage dressing table, laid out with wigs, jewels, headdresses, snake bracelets, snake earrings, and snake rings, a gold-beaded breastplate with Medusa's head carved in copper over the heart, lace-up leather Greek sandals, and a feathered, yellow-eyed, owl headdress. They were a vision of glorious raiments, all ready for the Goddess's grand entrance. But little did I know that my newest dance, Athena—Goddess of culture, wisdom, laws, and crafts—would prefigure what was to come on a global scale. On the evening of Saturday, September 9, 2001, the patron Goddess of the Amazons surged to life in my new concert, *Dances of the Silver*

Serpent.

Athena is the Greek Goddess of political strategy. She was considered a war Goddess by the patriarchal followers of the thunderbolt-wielding Zeus. It is commonly said that she sprung from the head of her father, Zeus, after he swallowed her mother Metis; however, some believe that Metis can be traced back to North Africa as Medusa, the powerful blood Goddess whose hair of writhing snakes symbolized her might and intelligence.

In her book *The Cult of Divine Birth in Ancient Greece*, Marguerite Rigoglioso posits that Athena was born parthenogenetically of her mother Metis. She also discusses Athena's relationship to the North African Amazons, whom she argues were historical priestesses.

I believe that Athena was born of Medusa in a "divine virgin birth." Not only was Medusa worn over Athena's heart on her breastplate, she was also emblazoned on Athena's shield. But her shield was not a shield at all. In my research, it was made out of goatskin, not a sturdy hide for use in war; however, goatskins make excellent drumheads.

I say that Athena was a dancing priestess who beat her drum to take people into ecstatic trance. She taught us about peace and prosperity through having us dance our truth, pounding out the rhythms of our hearts to synchronize ourselves to the One of Ones. I say Athena is a Goddess of liberation. She steps down from her chariot with her drum/shield of love and her ax/torch of truth. She is here forever and always—to protect us, guide us, and liberate us from our fears.

Athena, for whom the city of Athens was named, is also the Goddess of true democracy. As the overseer of the world's first democratic nation, she defends civilization. She was the first to tame the horse and invent the bridle and chariot. She is the strong, wise woman, virgin Goddess of peace.

As a woman moving into menopause, I was becoming virgin again. One unto myself, I would hold my wise blood within rather than bleed for humanity. The collective shadow of pain held by women that is released during menstruation would no longer bind me to this world. I could be in it but not of it. By no longer bleeding, I would be able to rise above the boundaries of gender and be defined by my personhood, not by my womanhood.

Athena, wise one, teacher of peace and prosperity, victorious overcomer of obstacles, be with me—I prayed—teach me to be fearless and lead me to truth and freedom. Oh, subduer of darkness, shield me with your love and liberate me with your labrys that I may dance in joy!

The program notes for the concert to honor the Goddess described 2001, the Year of the Silver Serpent:

> Snake years are said to herald dramatic events. During the last snake year, in 1989, we witnessed the tearing down of the Berlin Wall in Germany...The desires for material gain and status run strong this year and could result in manipulative or unscrupulous tactics. Scandal, strained relationships, environmental disasters, and international conflicts are all at the forefront. Watching the political arena, we are bearing witness to these negative patterns playing out before our very eyes...The Year of the Serpent is a time for revolutionary action and change. These dances are a celebration of the Year of the Silver Serpent and my artistic contribution toward healing the planet.

Every year has a specific energy with positive and negative possibilities. It can be used for both good and evil; it can be active or passive; and it can manifest as *yin* or *yang* or a blend of both.

Less than two days later, the twin towers of the World Trade Center were destroyed. Towers and obelisks represent the frozen serpent, *Kundalini* energy held in place. Metal and money are silver in physical form. Looking back now, I see the twin towers and the planes that hit them as aspects of the silver serpent energy, playing out negative patterns in the dramatic ways expected in Serpent Years.

A woman who had enjoyed my dance contacted me a few days after the performance and asked, "Who are you, Cassandra?" alluding to the ancient prophetess Cassandra's predictive ability and the World Trade Center tragedy that my program notes seemed to presage. At the time, I had just been embodying the Goddess the best I could. Had I, as Snake Priestess, acted as oracle, also?

During the performance, several difficulties arose—technical issues, videography problems—showing me that the Goddess was changing the show according to her will. She rearranged the order of the pieces by creating a situation that allowed no other options.

"Okay, Goddess," I surrendered.

Without hesitation, I grabbed the headset and dictated to the stage crew, "Guys, we're going straight through the show from here on. Lamia. Medusa. Athena. In that order. The Goddess says so."

My priestesses huddled around me, making decisions about how to get through all the costume changes effectively. Lights flashed, music blared, costumes flew, and priestesses prayed backstage. The warp and weave of the universe seemed to be unraveling, but I collected myself to walk out on stage as if nothing was wrong.

~

In full regalia, I stride out. An armored Amazon, I am ready to do righteous battle for the Goddess, my Mother. My drum, painted with an image of Medusa becomes my shield and the drumstick becomes my labrys, the double-bladed ax of peace and justice. The music hits a high note. I pound the drum furiously to awaken my audience. A call to action: Wake up! Don't go back to sleep! Wake up! Stand and be counted! I run in a spiral around and around, galloping on my stallion, then coil tightly into center, clenched fists, clenched jaws. I jump into a wide stance and pound the drum again. Now I am an activist—Athena, warrioress for peace and prosperity—asking: Will you come with me? Will you speak your truth?

~

The morning of 9/11, I was heading to Liam's school to drop him off. We made a quick detour to a neighborhood market to pick up some treats for him to take on a weeklong camping trip to Mount Lassen with his class. As I paid for the groceries, my eyes lifted to the wall-mounted television set, and Liam and I witnessed the oft-repeated footage of the planes assaulting New York City and the aftermath of the crumbling towers. I clutched my son's hand in mine as we watched the unbelievable events unfold.

At that very moment, my husband was driving south for a business trip. Soon, I would be alone, with my family gone, accompanied only by the panicked voices emanating from the TV. The paranoia perpetuated by the press threatened to overtake me.

That evening, to take a break from the barrage of information, I soaked in the hot tub. Sitting outside under the late summertime stars, I realized that something was missing: the usual nighttime noises of my town. The bridges around the county were closed. No airplanes flew overhead. No freeway noise. No children playing outside. It was a different world, as if it were holding its breath afraid to exhale. I figured that my neighbors, held hostage by an endless stream of news reports, were hiding in their homes.

I was grateful that our son was in nature, away from all the craziness. Though far apart, I knew we were both stargazing under the same sky. I ached with the separation from my loved ones. And then I thought of those who had lost their beloveds in this tragedy. All I could do was offer humble prayers for peace and understanding in this savage world.

I thought back to the moment in the concert when the universe seemed to be unraveling, when the Goddess wanted me to depict the three Goddesses Lamia, Medusa, and Athena as a trilogy. I understood now that they were related, and perhaps they themselves wanted to be known in order as the Triple Goddess: the grandmother/crone, the mother, and the daughter/maiden. Ending the show with the Minoan Snake Priestess as the oracle seemed perfectly ordained from on high.

This was the only concert with all my Snake Goddess dances highlighted in one show—a *tour de force*. I did not know it would be my last full concert, changing me forever not only in a personal sense but also in a global sense. September 11, 2001 changed everyone's life, and I couldn't help but wonder how Athena would alter me now that I had danced her.

Two days later, I received an email from a feminist scholar and author who had attended the concert: "If I had not seen your show I would not be able to bear this. Your dances have sustained me this week. They have given me faith that the

Goddess is coming in strong now to hold us during the collapsing artifices of patriarchal control."

Perhaps Athena was an advocate to accompany me in this new world. What I didn't know was how alone I would be in the coming times, and how I would have to stand on my own in my truth even more. Athena would help me become a spiritual warrioress on my own behalf, so that I truly would become "one unto myself."

Athena Dance – September 9, 2001

32

Twin Serpents

One afternoon, shortly after a therapy session in which memories of childhood sexual abuse had begun to surface, I developed a severe migraine headache. After a couple of doses of a homeopathic remedy and ibuprofen both failed to help, I remembered that Susan Weed, the Green Witch as she calls herself, recommended masturbation as a cure for migraines. Sometimes, when all else fails, going to the pleasure receptors in the body is the best way to alleviate pain. Made sense to me. Why not give it a try?

The afternoon sun dappled down through the trees, and the wind blew warmly. I lay down in the hammock in my garden under a shade tree next to the standing Quan Yin statue. She smiled serenely down at me and seemed to wink approval as I covered myself with a towel and slid my hands into my panties. At first, the pleasurable sensations felt soothing and calming. Suddenly these sensations changed into a burning hot stinging that was pulsing in each hip and in my sacrum.

When I looked into my hips with my inner eye to see what was causing this intense pain, I saw two snakes. The one at my left hip was white with black eyes, and the one on my right hip was black with white eyes. Their tails were intertwined at the base of my tailbone, and they repeatedly struck me. Over and over, their fangs sank into the flesh around my hips, creating the stinging sensation. I realized that the energy of these twin serpents was a living, yet impersonal knowing, inside me. When I looked at them, they seemed to say, "Get out of the way. Let us do our work."

The part of me that knows about soul retrieval in shamanic work and the wounded healer came forward as witness. I asked to be surrounded by the Goddess and her angels. I accepted the task before me and continued to masturbate even though the pain of the headache and the burning in my hips became excruciating. I reminded myself to follow my breath and let it flow as fully as I could throughout my whole body. The breath became a wave that I rode as if from way out in the wild sea into the crashing safety of the shoreline.

As I continued to breathe and stimulate myself, I was able to maintain multi-focused witnessing. My hips, my head, my vulva, my hands, and my breath all became focal points to hold attention and self-love. By now, the snakes had uncoiled and risen up into my abdomen, creating a fire in the belly. Waves of nausea and chills rippled through me simultaneously.

Suddenly, I was afraid that maybe I shouldn't be doing this alone. I had heard stories of people having *Kundalini* awakenings that sounded dangerous. And here I was, without the guidance of a trained professional. It was too late for that now, however, and somehow I knew that the only way out of this madness was to go through it. So I kept on going, trusting the wisdom of the body to unfold its healing journey.

I continuously reassured my little girl self that she was safe, and that we would emerge from this strange burning vision. I saw her as a luminous golden-white light shining in the dark—

Persephone holding a torch in the underworld. Such courage she had. I rested, breathing into the heart chakra with the two snakes becoming friendlier in their alchemical mating dance. They seemed happy to be set free and were no longer biting ferociously as if at war inside me but were staring into each other's eyes hypnotically entranced at my heart level where they had uncoiled and risen to face one another.

I rested here in the heart with the twin serpents. The nausea and chills were subsiding, but my head was pounding harder and hotter than before. I prayed to the Goddess for protection and guidance, asking for healing and grace. At that moment, the two snakes slithered smoothly through the small orifice of my throat like salmon swimming upstream to spawn. In an instant, they merged as one large eye in my brow chakra. The pupil of this eye was a *Yin-Yang* symbol. And the voice within my third eye said, "Within the darkness there is a speck of light, and within the light there is a speck of darkness. Let this be so inside you. Let the dualities of light and dark within you be married." As I surrendered to this, there was a rush of energy through my body. The *Yin-Yang* eye of the twin serpents spun through hidden doorways and passages inside me like a comet blazing a predestined course through the galaxy.

As the waves of pleasure engulfed my body, the emotional agony of awakened buried memories burst into consciousness. At that moment of orgasm, I saw myself as a little girl being coaxed into my uncle's bed and forced to accept his ejaculating phallus in my mouth. This changed quickly to images of Christ on the Cross and bloodthirsty Kali Ma. These deities floated in my psyche as potent symbols to hang my sanity on. My crown chakra blew open like a super nova—the universe being created, the moment of the big bang. Gasping sounds I had never heard myself make were coming out of my mouth. Tears were streaming down my cheeks, and I thrashed in the hammock like a fish caught in a net.

The inner voices said, "It is done my child. So be it." The orgiastic snake ritual inside me was over. I lay still, breathing hard, my headache gone. My eyes were rolled back into my head, gazing up at my third eye. The door to the top of my head was open, and from it poured a milky white stream of consciousness. I was Lord Shiva in a blissful swoon. Ecstatic Kali Ma, a dancing *dakini* above me, held my severed head in her hand, delighted to add it to her collection of sacred treasures around her neck. My breath nearly ceased as it deepened into that sweet yogic space of almost no breath. I fell into a drunken slumber.

When I woke, it seemed as though months had passed by. All the intense pain was gone, and even the ecstasy had faded. I felt like a wrung-out towel—everything twisted out of me in both directions. I staggered out of the hammock, across the lawn, up onto the deck, and into the house. I looked at the clock. Only three hours had passed.

33

Snake Path

> Falling tears
>   Falling rain
>   Falling façades
> A pouring out of love
>   A renewal of my spirit
>   A revival of the land
>   Softening
>   Surrender
>   Solace
>
> —Le'ema

Now that I knew what had happened to me as a child, it was time to speak my truth—to open the lid I had put on myself. For years I had been silent. The kind of disabling silence that keeps a woman locked down. I remember asking the Sufi Master one time how personal power related to spiritual power. His answer then was, "There is no such thing as personal power, that is only the negative ego. Spiritual power is all there is."

I wondered now how many gurus have said that to their female students just to keep them quiet. It certainly confused me at the time. How could a teacher advocate celibacy when he himself was receiving sexual favors from many of his female students? I left the retreat angry that year, swearing to never return.

But here I was, back again for three weeks, with strengthened resolve to speak to him. It had taken twenty years to summon the strength of mind I needed to risk his disapproval. To my knowledge, no one had ever confronted him.

A new friend, Shanti, an older woman who was a therapist and had not until then heard of the teacher's exploits, encouraged me. She gave me this advice, "Your power is in the sacred triangle of your vulva and hips. As a belly dancer you know this. Hold your feminine ground, and do not let his masculine ego topple you." With her hands on her hips she continued, "And just remember three things to say: This is what happened to me. This is how it affected me. And this is what I need you to hear."

Shanti was a goddess-send. Her wise crone strength gave me the courage to carry on. I decided to speak to him that very day. I hadn't been able to broach the subject with him earlier but would leave tomorrow, so this was my last chance. I had to speak the truth.

In order to ground myself with some Mexican soul food, I headed to the nearest local dive forty-five miles away. Three weeks on a bland vegetarian diet had not been stabilizing. As I drove, I chanted in Arabic the whole time. *"Ya Malik,"* repeated to earn respect and be treated accordingly by others, is one of the ninety-nine Names of Allah, meaning Sovereign Lord.

At the cantina, I ordered tacos and a Coke, and while I was waiting, I wrote in my journal the things I wanted to say. When my food came, I enjoyed every morsel. The beef tacos smothered with cheese, guacamole, and jalapeno salsa gave me just the right stamina I needed for my task. A full belly soothed my jangled nerves.

Big thunderheads were quickly rolling in when I got back to my car, but I was the calm before the storm. I drove back down the dirt road to the center, happy to see the bright orange orb setting in the azure sky and the wondrous gathering of the lightning snakes and thunderbirds that bring the rains.

When I stepped off the plane on this trip in the month of July, the sky was hazy, and a hot wind was blowing smoke from the wildfires in Arizona and Colorado. I was distressed that my New Mexico sky was so sad and the earth, so parched. And news reports indicated that the fires were approaching the mountains here. As soon as I was on the open highway in the rental car, my rain prayers began and continued every day for the time that I was there. Within forty-eight hours of my arrival, precipitation made its first appearance. Every afternoon it would come—a gentle She shower one day or a fierce warrior flood the next. The Land of Enchantment would be renewed and so would my spirit.

Back at the center, I parked the car and ran to my cabin to change clothes. As I bounded along the rocky path, a little yellow and gray striped garter snake appeared to guide my way. She slithered quickly ahead of me all the way to the door of the cabin and then vanished. I put on a T-shirt painted in vibrant colors with two snakes encircling tantric lovers from various world cultures and threw a pink sweater around my shoulders. Then I carefully retraced my steps back along the trail and hiked up to the cabin where my teacher resided.

A young female student answered the door. I requested to see the teacher and was left standing on the steps of the rickety wooden porch. Soon he appeared. He did not invite me in but came outside to join me.

"I need to talk to you," I said.

He took a step backwards. "Okay, go ahead."

I cleared my throat, took a big breath, and sent my grounding cord down into the earth. "It's important that you know that the sexual interlude that happened between us twenty-three years ago was inappropriate. I need you to know how it affected me. When you gave me that so-called massage, it was not love to me, or even a promise of good sex. You rolled on top of me, without giving me a moment to consent!"

I didn't dare use the words date rape, though years before, when I told my husband about it, that's what he called it. But the memory of him jerking my left leg nearly out of its socket and heaving himself on me with his hot, stale breath has never left me.

"I don't do that anymore," he said. "I—"

"Let me finish," I inserted. "I came to someone I trusted in good faith to find my soul but ended up being seduced by the very person I trusted to protect me. It left a black spot on me that I want to cleanse and heal. I will always love you as my first spiritual teacher, but I will never totally trust you. I don't want to carry this pain of betrayal around with me any longer, so I give it back to you!"

I gestured to him with both palms up as though handing him a heavy suitcase filled with the disgust of all the women he ever mistreated, then took a deep, slow breath in and waited for his response.

"I don't do that anymore," he repeated. "I am not interested in sex at all. I am only interested in purity. Sex is a distraction. It can only bring the energy down."

I looked at the ground, feeling uncomfortable with his holier-than-thou pretense. Why couldn't he just admit that he was a fallible human being? But I squeamishly shuffled my feet in the dirt and let him go on his spiritual rant. I knew I wouldn't hear an apology from him. This was as close to an "I'm sorry" as I would ever get.

Meanwhile, the sky became completely overcast. When he finished his lecture, I felt oddly relieved. I went on to tell him that one month before coming to camp, I had discovered the sexual abuse from my childhood. The memories had finally surfaced after two years of therapy. I told him how it made me feel ambivalent about my sexuality. I started to cry. He stood there in his white yoga clothes (which had earned him the nickname of the ice cream man) and studied me with pensive dark eyes.

Everything became quiet. Still. I felt his heart open to me in a compassionate holding space. Moisture swelled the air. Suddenly, with a bolt of lightning and a crash of thunder, the clouds burst and the rains pelted us.

The teacher grabbed an umbrella and put his arm around me. We walked briskly, clamored together, down to the meditation hall, where he insisted that I sit next to him on the stage. Then he introduced me to the group. "This is Scheherazade," he said, calling me by my secret name. "She is a Sufi teacher. Tonight she will lead us in the chant, 'Shafi', which means to heal." Although he had previously asked me to teach on different occasions, I was flustered by the unexpected timing. We chanted for the whole evening as the He rains turned to She rains. When the chant drifted off into ensuing silence, the rain stopped.

After dinner and farewells to friends, I padded back up the hill to my cabin under a clear sky. I felt open and expanded. At last, at ease. Snuggled in my sleeping bag, I mused whether the Sufi master's fear of his own mortality translated into a rapacious appetite for women that was seeded in an unconscious desire to find a lineage-holder since he himself had been trained by his mother and grandmother.

I peered out the window at a tall Ponderosa pine. Through its branches, thousands of stars glittered above in the black canopy. As I floated off to sleep, I wondered if this was my thousandth and one night.

Although I have continued to study with some of the finest in the tradition, I never took up the mantle of "Sufi Teacher." It is enough for me to simply be as dervish, a priestess.

Six years later, the Sufi center burned to the ground, swallowed by wildfires. To me, the fires were the physical and symbolic manifestation of the collective unexpressed female rage that had seeped into the very foundation of the land.

34

Return of the Snakes

It was March 17, 2002, just a few months after the 9/11 tragedy. St. Patrick, traditionally celebrated on this day, was said to have driven the snakes out of Ireland. Since there never were indigenous snakes in Ireland, we know that driving the snakes out meant that he was actually ridding Ireland of its elders, druids, and earth-based spiritual traditions so that the Catholic Church would have power over the people. Today, many pagans choose to celebrate differently by calling the wisdom of the serpents back.

I was invited to be the mascot for the *Return of the Snakes* Pagan Pride Parade in downtown Berkeley.

Élan had gone to UC Berkeley in the 70s and had fond memories of the creative chaos and the exuberant aura of the community. When we had gotten together in the 80s, I lived in the area. Our first date had been in one of the ethnic restaurants that dot the scene there. We looked forward to this day to revel in our lost youth.

We were disappointed in the changes we saw. Where once these buildings carried an aliveness, a thriving bigness, they now seemed small, provincial, and dingy. Élan and I had often walked down these sidewalks, feeling them full of promise. People's Park was no longer a haven for the homeless, but a cesspool of those left behind from a bygone era. The street people seemed old and tired, no more flower power left in them.

That misty March morning, I sat on the sunroof of our car feeling like a queen, my long, green snake tail spiraled around me in a coil. Élan, wearing a Green Man mask, sat in the driver's seat, waiting for the parade to move along Telegraph Avenue. I smiled and waved at the people as they passed. They waved back with a question in their eyes. *Could I—their queen—save them?*

Leaning my face down to Élan, I asked, "Does this make you feel young or old?"

"Both," he replied.

My gaiety hid feelings of nostalgia. I sighed out loud, longing, longing, longing. *Would any of us ever return to that land of the free? Of innocence? Of hope?*

It was cold and damp sitting on top of the car with just my snake suit on. It had rained all morning, and I needed some sunshine to warm my bones. I gazed up at the clouds and sent a silent prayer that the rain would end and let us have our parade. I reminisced about the dances that Élan and I had performed together over the years, especially *The Green Man and the Serpent in the Garden,* and how our passion for the sacred in sexuality had always been reflected in our choreographies.

Seated as the Queen of the Snakes on the throne of our VW Jetta, I reveled in the chaos of the parade and the people on the streets. Indeed, the Goddess Fortuna had smiled on me in my life, and I now could see how lucky I had been. My Green Man, my husband Élan, has been a perfect partner in the unfolding of my destiny as a modern day Snake Priestess. His willingness to dance with me, both literally and spiritually, on this path has been a gift of fertility and abundance for us both.

It had been thirteen years since our rainy wedding day. Our son, our snake baby, a thriving twelve-year-old, rode alongside the car on his electric scooter with a lime green, stuffed snake wrapped around the handlebars. He was content, at least, to be part of the menagerie that is our family.

Though I felt great happiness for the good fortune that the rain had showered upon us at our wedding, today's rain was somber. It made me feel cold and sad. The street people, lonely and homeless, dirty and sick, seemed to be enduring a suffering that flooded the entire world—the human condition of perennial pain. What could they do, these dank dwellers? Where would they go?

From the recesses of my Catholic school choir days, a hymn formed on my lips. Even before I knew what I was singing, the *Salve Regina* silently poured out of my mouth. With all of my heart, I implored her...

> Hail Holy Queen, Mother of Mercy
> Our Life, our sweetness and our hope
> To Thee do we cry
> Poor banished children of Eve
> To Thee do we send up our sighs, mourning and weeping in this valley of tears...

A faint smell of roses wafted past me, the invisible perfume of Mother Mary.

The parade marshal gave the signal for us to move. As soon as the car started, the clouds parted and a brilliant shaft of pink sunlight shot through. There, standing in radiance was Mary.

She stretched out her hands toward me and spoke, "Ah my child..."

A sob welled up in my chest. *Oh, my Goddess! She's here! She's really here!*

Mary stood in her raiment of light, an iridescent pinkish white robe covered with a heavenly blue cape and a pearl-white veil on her head. She smiled sweetly down upon me with eyes pouring out love—grace, eminent grace.

"My daughter, I am here for you," she said, "I reveal myself to you in this form because you already know my truth in your being." She lifted her skirt to display the serpent at her feet, coiled around her ankles. She held a white dove nestled in the palms of both hands at her heart.

She began to shape-shift into one aspect of the Goddess after another: Aphrodite, Kali, the Black Madonna, Isis, Artemis, Hecate, Quan Yin, Medusa, Demeter, Parvati, Green Tara, Brigid, Lamia, Sheila-Na-Gig, Ma'at, Hathor, Our Lady of Guadalupe, Mary Magdalena, Astarté, the Minoan Snake Goddess, Lilith, Inanna, Freya. Hundreds, no thousands, of Goddesses emanated through her at the speed of light, morphing from one to the next.

She was blindingly beautiful. Each time I felt even the slightest doubt arise as to why she was displaying Herself to me this way, Mary would say, "Because, my child, you know me, and because you have always thought me near, I am here now."

Then she did the most astonishing thing. She started laughing, a laughter that roared a thunderous *Hallelujah* inside my body, vibrating to my very DNA. With one lilting movement of her hands, she raised the dove to her heart and released it. The dove flew toward me, disappearing into my third eye and descending inside me to my heart. I felt my heart explode into a cosmic rainbow of swirling colors and light. I thought I would faint and fall off the car, but I maintained my composure somehow and continued smiling and waving to the crowds in the streets as though nothing out-of-the-ordinary had occurred.

Then she did yet another astonishing thing: she reached down with both hands, and in one quick motion, whisked off her garment to reveal her naked body! When she removed her veil, out tumbled luscious long hair the color of burnished copper, which fell nearly to her thighs. At that moment, she again opened the palms of her hands, streaming forth golden-white beams of light to give a blessing.

The serpent at her feet, an emerald green tree boa, slithered up her left leg, spiraling its way up and around her body till it came to rest over her right shoulder. It planted its head on her heart above her left breast, flicking its tongue over the pink areola and nipple. Our Lady looked down with a knowing smile at her serpent friend. Then, tossing her head, her long, luscious locks formed a halo around her face. Our Lady picked up the serpent's head and held it in her hands and kissed it. At that moment, the dove resting inside my heart fluttered down into my belly, into my womb, and flew out my yoni. It circled me three times and flew off into the distance beyond Mary.

The scene behind Mary, like time-lapse photography, grew into a wild garden, lush with tropical fruit trees, flowers, date palms, orchids, and ferns. The animals came to join her in a menagerie of wild life: deer, mountain lions, monkeys, bats, elephants, spiders. A waterfall appeared, flowing with fresh, cool water. An apple tree loaded with golden fruit stood in the foreground. Our Lady walked over to it, picked one of the apples, and bit into the crisp skin. She reached out, motioning for me to take a bite, too.

In that instant, everything swirled inward. My pupils contracted and closed. She was gone. But her voice echoed after...

> Return again
> Return again
> Return to the land of the wild divine.
> Come to my garden of primordial delight
> Yours evermore,

Eva,
Eva Maria

Return of the Snakes

Le'ema as Queen of the Snakes leading the Pagan Pride Parade

35

Brigid ~ Ireland ~ Roots

                    Brig
                Bride   Brite
            Brighid   Brigantia
        Brigda   Briget
        Bride   Brigda
        Birdhid   Bridgid
        Brigantia   Brighde
        Brigandu   Briggidda
            Bridey   Bridge
                Brigit   Brigitte
                    Sun
                    Star
                    Fire
                    Light
                    Moon
                    Blood
                    Dream
                    Healer
                    Holy Well

—Le'ema

I often felt weepy and homesick among photographs of the vast blue-grey-green sea, rocky cliffs, and outcroppings of Ireland. What was this longing to find my roots, my tribe, my people? Was it because I never knew my family history? Was it mere fantasy to connect with the magical mythology from the past, where Druids built stone circles and followed the movement of constellations and fairies made flowers bloom, drinking the morning dewdrops as nectar of immortal life? And what exactly was I looking for? Would it surface in the rivers of Liffe, Boynbe, Bride, or Shannon? Or perhaps it would be found in the Cliffs of Moher, towering citadels overlooking the expansive ocean to the Aran Islands. Would I see my tribe in the myriad of butterflies or dragonflies of scarlet orange and cerulean blue? Or in the shamrocks, rainbows, cairns, and castles?

In August of 2006, Élan and I traveled to Ireland with Liam, now a tall, gracefully thin, sixteen-year-old. More than a vacation, this trip was a pilgrimage to visit Lady Olivia Robertson at her castle in Clonegal. As it turned out, it was also a time of acknowledging my next phase in the life cycle—a time to say goodbye to my youth and hello to my roots.

A few months before the trip, I had been doing research on my maternal line and discovered that my mother had an older half-sister, an aunt who I knew nothing about. They had never met, and somehow, this woman had become a broken branch on the family tree. Perceived as an outcast in my extended family, I felt inexplicably entangled with this lost aunt who was rumored to have become a writer. I looked everywhere to find records of her, to no avail.

To process this loss, I attended a therapeutic workshop on family constellations in the hope of healing a family that was missing part of its structure. In some ways, though, it seemed no amount of work would seal the divide between my family and me. They were different, parked in El Paso, while I felt like a true-blood Celt, with more of a connection to the Ancient Ones than my own birth family.

The facilitator, Brigitte, asked participants in the workshop to be representatives of my family going back as far as my great, great, great grandmother. Five women were lined up behind me with their hands on each other's shoulders and mine, offering the support of a healed and complete female lineage. I could feel the spiral of my mother line, starting with my missing Aunt Mary and her sister, my mother, Laurah Jane and her mother, Nellie Viola, and her mother, Laura Bell, and her mother, and her mother, all the way back to the Great Mother Herself. The result was empowering and uplifting. Afterwards, I felt ready to embark on a long-overdue expedition to the birthplace of my ancestors.

With the stress of packing for the trip, I didn't pay attention to the mysterious blood spot in my underwear. *I'm already in menopause,* I thought and accepted that occasional spotting was probably normal. But to my shock, by the time we crossed the Atlantic Ocean, it had evolved into a full-on period. A major hormonal shift was culminating in my body. I didn't know that in Ireland I would bid farewell to my moon, offering my last blood to the Ancient Ones.

After a long nap in our Dublin bed and a full Irish breakfast, Élan asked, "Where shall we begin our journey?"

In need of comfort and healing, I responded, "Let's find Brigid, I want to be on her land."

I understood that the Goddess, Brigid, was associated with fertility, healing, and snakes, but I had no idea that she was associated with blood. One of her names, "Bright," links her to "Star Fire," said to be the life-giving properties of the Goddess' divine menstrual blood or "alchemical gold." And here I was, bleeding my way through Eire!

So, in the afternoon of our first day on the Emerald Isle, we drove to Kildare to locate the sites sacred to this pre-eminent deity/saint of Celtic healing. Some say Brigid—the daughter of a Druid—was baptized by St. Patrick. After a lifetime of sublime service as an abbess, she was canonized as a saint. Others say she is a great archetypal Goddess. And then there are those who see her as both. Many sacred sites of the Goddess became dedicated to St. Brigid after the spread of Christianity in Ireland. To this day, pagan ceremonies and Christian practices have co-existed in the Irish community, which celebrate her as an indigenous spirit.

St. Brigid's Day, February 1st, shows her to be an aspect of the Snake Goddess. This holiday is the basis for the American Groundhog Day, when she, as a snake, emerges from her mound, marking the first day of Celtic Spring. In one ritual, a silk headband known as a *ribin* is left overnight to grow longer, representing the Snake Goddess in her linear role as healer.

For me, Brigid, whose name means "Exalted One," is implicitly associated with shamanism. There is a direct connection between shamans and poets worldwide. Transformers of culture, poets are the shamans of language. Because she is the muse of poets and writers, I brought the unfinished parts of my manuscript to be blessed at her sites around the island.

Bucolic and secluded, Brigid's Holy Well is truly the most sacrosanct place I have ever set foot upon. It is lush, green, and brimming with curative forces. Kneeling before the well, I placed my book down. As I asked for healing of my womb, the wind blew open the pages to the chapter *Becoming a Snake Priestess*. The words "almost bleeding to death" jumped out at me. It felt like so much more than coincidence. I placed some of her holy water on my head, heart, and womb and sprinkled a few drops on my book.

It is said that Brigid represents the three sacred fires: the Heart, for inspiration; the Hearth, for healing; and the Forge, for transformation. Our next stop was St. Brigid's Cathedral, the home of her restored fire pit. A perpetual fire had once burned on these grounds, tended by Brigid and her nineteen priestesses who made sure the light was never extinguished. I stepped down inside this subterranean space, holding my book, and beseeched Brigid to inspire, heal, and transform me.

We also visited the Hill of Tara, the seat of sacred kingship and a hallowed dwelling place of Gods and Goddesses such as Lugh and Maeve, both intimately associated with sovereignty. As we hiked the long path leading to the hill, I came upon a large statue of St. Patrick. The Druids—referred to as "snakes"—were driven out of Ireland by St. Paddy. In my best Irish accent, I flippantly told him, "Just be lettin' you know, I'm bringing the snakes back." At the summit, where one can see half the counties in Ireland, the Ancient Ones held me strong. I pressed my manuscript to my chest and embraced the renowned *Lia Fa'il*—The Stone of Destiny—my cloak flapping in the winds. It was as if the stone wanted to be heard, not merely seen. I had once read that only true kings could hear its roar, yet the great phallic rock bellowed inside me body! By that evening, the surprise surge of menstrual blood had fulfilled its final cycle.

It wasn't until later in the trip that Lady Olivia told me: "Grahams were the rightful kings of England."

I found my family coat of arms in a tourist shop in Kenmare. Beneath the motto, "free and erect," I silently read the passage to myself.

"William de Graham was a Norman baron believed to be the original bearer of the name," I announced to Élan and Liam. "That was my grandfather's name!"

The Grahams were a band of travelers, one of the most powerful of the outlaw "riding clans," having migrated to the Scottish borders in the 17th century. They then migrated to Northern Ireland and are now mostly located in Ulster and Dublin. Graham now ranks among the hundred commonest surnames in Ireland.

We also noticed that there were Grahams in Dingle Peninsula when we found the name on a plaque outside of O'Flaherty's Pub one evening. Of course, we had to go in. The owner, O'Flaherty himself, was serenading everyone with a ballad. My family celebrated into the wee hours with the ebullient and boisterous pub-crawlers, listening to the spirited Irish tunes. I closed my eyes and inhaled the sound. Ears as a pathway spiral to the soul! The music circled my heart all the way down to my belly, then down into my tailbone, through my feet and into the earth like a long snake rooting me to the land of my blood, welcoming me home.

When I was pregnant with Liam, my root chakra would vibrate whenever I heard Irish music. The forlorn sound of the *uilleann pipes* would make me weep. But here, in this pub, the joyful jigs and reels played by the lively *bodhran*, penny whistles, fiddles, and flutes stirred my emotions and roused my spirits. My musical son learned to play the fiddle on that vacation, even performing with a group of Irish musicians after we returned home.

We arrived at our final destination in the late afternoon: Lady Olivia's castle. I was eager to know more about the woman who captured our imaginations with her crossed eye, high accent, and eccentric ways. In her 90s, Lady Olivia is an enchantress sublime, never to be called crone, yet as venerable as the history and the shrines contained within her castle walls.

We were exhausted from many hours cramped in our wee car driving around the Emerald Isle, and yet I could not refuse Lady Olivia's request that I dance between the scenes of a mystery play. She also asked Liam to participate as the lead. He obliged, willing to play the handsome hero and bless us all with his graceful presence and elegant voice. We were the American stars in the show directed by our perfect hostess, Gwendoline, an Irish woman who recognized me as kin through our priestess lineage.

Truthfully, it was all rather chaotic and silly. I scrambled through my luggage to find something that resembled dancing costumes. Luckily, my iPod was loaded with lovely music, so I chose six different tunes to inspire the dance. It was a challenge, but somehow the skill of improvisation carried me through in magical ways. The performance, held in a theatre that had once been a carriage house, came off with as much *panache* as we could muster, to the delight of Lady Olivia and her small group of local friends. Perhaps the faery folk themselves gave me back my dancing feet. I felt like Yeats' *Sweet Dancer, come to many a Danaan shore to dance for his Old Queen Maeve…*

Afterwards, we celebrated at the town pub. Lady Olivia entertained us all with wild tales of her encounters with ghosts and crazy men.

It was late into the evening when I was finally able to relax in a warm bubble bath, surrounded by candles. We stayed in Gwendoline's modern townhouse, just five minutes from the castle. I had never been so thankful for creature comforts! Cozy in an Irish lace and linen bed, I wrote in my journal, pondering my admonishment to St. Patrick. It would take awhile to grasp that by simply having brought my son here, I had already returned the serpent. Two years later, Liam visited Ireland on his own, immersing himself in the culture and music of our ancestors. He was indeed the snake—the son of a Druidess returned.

For reasons I couldn't explain, I had always felt the need to see Ireland before visiting other countries. Now, with my ancestral roots grounded beneath me, I was free to grow and expand, branching out into a world of possibilities.

Le'ema in Ireland at St. Brigid's Well

Brigid's Fire Temple

Lady Olivia's Huntington Castle, Clonegal
Original Illustration by Michael Howes

New Grange

36

Sekhmet ~ Egypt ~ Stars

I stood between the paws of the Sphinx—the great cat—keeper of secrets from time beyond time. We were asked to select a Neter card from Nicki's *Anubis Oracle* deck. I drew Anubis himself, the black jackal-headed guide of the underworld.

This felt ominous since the first thing I had seen upon setting foot on the Giza plateau that foggy dawn was a black dog. Somehow I knew then that this trip to Egypt would be a journey like no other. Even so, I was not prepared for the adventures before me. I had worked with many of the Egyptian Neteru in trainings with Nicki and in the Temple of Isis with Lady Loreon and Lady Olivia, yet I had never traveled to the Black Land to experience these powerful deities of the Egyptian pantheon.

I wasn't confident that I wanted to be with Anubis, the God of embalming and mummification, also known as guide and friend to the dead. My ego needed to be comfortable; it didn't want to face the unknown. Ugh. I didn't want to visit the depths of the underworld, I wanted to have an upper world journey!

The following morning while waiting for the bus, I told Nicki that I really wanted to work with the protector Goddess, Wadjet.

She looked at me quizzically. "Le'ema how many years have you been working with Wadjet? Eighteen? Twenty? More?" She laughed out loud. "You know her already. It's time for a new Neter."

I admitted that I was afraid of dying.

"Well, you're in the wrong place then," she said. "This will be a shamanic death. See it as an exquisite melt down, as the key to expanding into the NOW moment of total presence where you can see forward, backward, and all of time. See from all views. You're a Snake Priestess! Shed the stories that define you to become the consciousness that you ARE."

She placed her hands on my shoulders. "You can do this, Le'ema. Anubis is the epitome of loving kindness. Just let go, and you will be protected."

I looked at her with the eyes of a totally trusting child, then ran off to do yoga on the grass beneath a palm tree. As I pressed my palms down on the earth and pushed my heels back into downward facing dog pose, I prayed, "Oh, Anubis, I honor you. Take care of me 'cause I'm a newbie."

Later, I would learn that Anubis was thought to have a daughter, Kebechet, who was depicted as a snake carrying water. She was the Goddess of freshness and purification through water, bringing that sacred water to Anubis for his tasks. She washed the entrails of the deceased and gave water to the spirits of the dead to fortify their bodies against corruption while they waited for the mummification process to be complete.

We boarded the bus to go to the oldest step pyramid, Saqarra, and drove through an increasingly lush countryside. Egypt truly was the desert oasis that all the books had described. At the sight of grove upon groves of date palms, I was overcome with emotion and thrown back into an ancient time. I began to weep uncontrollably and felt that if I died today, it would be okay. And I did die that day inside the step pyramid. During the guided journey beside an abyss at the end of a long tunnel, I watched myself being dismembered, torn to shreds, and devoured by a wild beast. This was too violent for my sensitive nature. While others seemed to go on without consequence, it knocked me off my equilibrium and plunged me into what I now understand was destructive.

That night, we boarded the overnight train to Aswan. My stomach was feeling funny, and sure enough, I had contracted Mummy's Tummy. Just my luck to be up down, up down, up down, all through the night. The only good thing about my trips to the toilet was peering out the windows to see the long serpent of the Nile float past me.

At some point I slept, dreaming I was Anubis wrapped as a mummy and suspended upside down from my feet that were tied together by a snake on the world tree. Just when the train made a jerking movement and stopped, I was cut from the tree and slipped silently into the deep, dark waters below. I woke with a start and knew for sure I was in over my head. The descent into the underworld and my ensuing demise seemed certain.

When we arrived in Aswan, I was given a private room and medicine for the microbials. Yet I continued to become feverish and depleted. In the exquisite garden of our island resort overlooking the Nile, I lay down next to Nicki. She stroked my head while we shared what had happened during our journeys in the step pyramid.

"It was appropriate to have Anubis as my guide," I confessed to the group, "since I was 'sick as a dog.'"

I went on to speak of my journey with two Anubis jackals on either side of me, one white and one black, and how they told me I was balancing my soul with Ma'at, the Egyptian Goddess of justice who weighs the heart of the deceased on her scales against her feather of truth.

Nicki said, "You've passed the test!"

When I stood up to walk back to my room, I fainted, feeling myself slip through the cracks, through the veils of time. Before I hit the ground, two Nubian men dashed over and scooped me up into their arms. They carried me like an Egyptian queen on a dais and took me to a side room of the hotel where I began to babble, *"Sa Sekhem Sahu, Sa Sekhem Sahu, Sa Sekhem Sahu."* Then, laughing like a crazy woman, I murmured, "That's the only Egyptian magic I know."

Nicki led me back to my room. She wanted to give me antibiotics, but I refused. They sent someone from our group, a nurse, to check me out. It turned out I had fainted because of dehydration. The nurse suggested adding salt to the water to help balance my electrolytes. One of the men, Mohamed, made sure I had Egyptian lemonade, chicken soup, and potato chips, then tucked me into bed. I loaded myself up with homeopathic remedies and slept until our 3:00 a.m. wake up call. This was the day I had been waiting for, and there was no way I was going to miss it.

Nicki knocked on my door, looking a little surprised to see me with make-up on and my hair fixed, wearing a purple robe over a galabaya. I rushed with her down to the boat and jumped in with everyone. Nicki asked if I wanted to dance, and of course, I agreed.

One of the other leaders inquired, "Are you sure? You've been so sick."

"Isis will heal me. I shall dance her. You'll see," I responded.

I clicked on my iPod and, magically, the tune "Amber," by Light Rain, appeared without my having to go through the play list. It had to be a sign from Isis; she wanted me to dance to that song.

When we arrived, it was pitch black. We were asked to wait in silence as Nicki prepared the temple for ceremony. But I leapt off the boat, following Nicki straight to the inner sanctum of the temple. It was as if my feet had traversed these grounds hundreds of times before. Nicki set the sacred objects on the stone altar, then handed me a vial of rose oil and asked me to anoint my fellow pilgrims as they entered. Soon everyone filtered in through the mist for a short prayer offering ceremony.

We processed to the outer temple courtyard where we sat on the edge of the old stone walls and watched the sunrise over the Nile. The light of the sun pierced my third eye, filling me with bliss. While everyone meditated, Nicki led me to the temple steps where I assumed the classic pose of Isis, one knee down and one up. The group turned to face me as Nicki announced, "Behold the Goddess."

I danced Isis in the most sacred way I could, opening my robe like wings and moving from side to side in profile with the same posture as Isis on her Temple Walls. She gave blessings through my hands to our group, to the Nile and her people, and to the whole world. When the music ended, I invited the group to dance to a more lively and upbeat tune. Everyone was joyous and danced entranced to our lady Isis. Her magnificent wings enfolded all of us as we worshipped her in the ancient way through music and dance and celebration. I was home at last.

Later, I explored the temple on my own, still wobbly and vulnerable, but with a great sense of knowing in my body. One of the guards playfully made a turban on my head with my scarf. We had been warned not to let the guards distract us with ploys for tips, but I knew I was safe. I had died with Anubis guiding me in the underworld where his father, Osiris, presided over death to be reborn in the wings of Isis, She of Ten Thousand Names.

The next day we boarded a ship for our cruise down the Nile. Our first stop was the Kom Ombo temple of Healing. Nicki guided us in a powerful ritual of embracing and holding the tension of duality within ourselves. We walked to the temple in two lines, chanting "Sobek, Horus." One side represented Sobek, the crocodile-headed God, and the other side Horus, the hawk-headed God. Sobek represented the reptilian brain and Horus the neo-cortex, or the lower and higher brains. I, of course, was chosen for the Sobek side, given my love of reptiles. In our shamanic journey, we were guided down into a water pit to swim with the crocodiles to help us overcome our fear of death. I happily went splashing down since I had always liked crocodiles and saw myself swim safely up and out the hidden chamber.

On the other side of the temple was a very deep well where the ancient Egyptians kept a crocodile in honor of Sobek. As I peered over the edge to look down into the well, my upper abdomen quivered. My solar plexus, right below my sternum bone, pulled me like a magnet to the other side of the temple. There, carved on one of the walls, was a large image of Sobek wearing Hathor's crown. Hathor's crown!

I collapsed, sliding down the wall in a complete loss of coherence. A body memory flashed through me. As a child, my head got stuck between the pillars of a circular pool where crocodiles were kept in the center of the plaza in downtown El Paso. I must have been only four or five years old and was innocently peering in at them when one of the crocodiles started coming toward me with his huge jaws. Petrified, I couldn't get my head out. My mom and my aunt were walking away, and the big creature was coming to eat me. I was crying and screaming; finally, my Aunt came and freed me by twisting my head out.

Ever since then, I had been captivated by crocodiles and had gradually grown to appreciate them in adulthood, especially the way they could slip into deep hibernation when cold. No wonder I loved Steve Irwin, the Crocodile Hunter.

But to see Hathor's crown on Sobek just undid me. I wondered if Sobek had conquered Hathor, or if she had tamed him and taught him to love so that he deserved to wear her crown of fourteen cobras with the solar and lunar disc. As a woman, I have loved being devoured by certain lovers. What is this feminine need to give all, to be consumed by Love? How I love disappearing into the passion of being taken. And because I serve Hathor, Goddess of love and sacred sexuality, it all made sense now. So I wept at the bas relief of Sobek, in awe of the raw primal power of lust and love and the great healing potential that exists therein. Hathor, as the Goddess of Love, teaches us to tame the beast of Lust and lure him into raising his *Kundalini* to become the God of Love. I have learned how to tame the beast.

My body was completely changed after this experience, and the change has lasted. It seemed as if the *bandha*, the lock between my solar plexus and my heart, was opened so that the energy of my belly and my power could merge with my heart as my truth. Power and will, united with the love and compassion of the heart, make one a true spiritual warrioress.

We headed back to the boat for dinner and sailed on to Edfu. That night, for our visit to the temple of Horus, I donned a black galabaya with pink lotuses on the sleeves. What powerful magic in this temple! I felt my priestess/lover/goddess self rise, rise, rise and join with all the great spirits here. I moved up to the front in the inner sanctum with the other priestesses as we sang and chanted, "My heart, my mother, my heart, my mother, my heart of my becoming." I held the space between the solar barque of Hathor and Horus and the sanctuary. It was a potent moment. My feet were planted as if I had been standing there as priestess forever. We felt our hearts recharge as we faced the scarab inscribed on the wall behind the holy of holies. When the rite ended, I shook my sistrum and danced and whirled with delight at the union of the God and Goddess. I remembered the joy I had felt many years ago dancing Hathor and Horus, the divine lovers, with my husband to Nicki's guided visualization at the Convocation of Isis at the Temple of Isis, and later, at the Pantheacon event in San Francisco where I was the bare-breasted love goddess. And again, today in this temple, their love and joy returned me to myself. We sailed on to Luxor, our last destination on the Nile River.

At Karnak, the grand temple built by Ramses II, there was a secret side chapel with three rooms. Sekhmet, the Lion headed mother of Egypt stands before the side chapel as the only "living" statue left in the temples of Egypt. This eight-foot tall unblemished basalt statue has reigned here for at least 3,500 years. So strong is her energy that it was as if the statue itself were alive. Her eyes seemed to stare right into my soul as she stood, with the breasts of a woman, holding a lotus staff in one hand and an ankh in the other. She spoke directly through me: "If you want my power, suckle at my breast." I laughed, knowing full well that I couldn't do this in front of everyone who was waiting in line behind me.

After touring the main temple, I meandered back over to the chapel and asked the guard for a private entrance, giving him a handsome baksheesh of a hundred Egyptian pounds, the equivalent of twenty U.S. dollars. The tip assured me solo time with this beloved lioness, crowned with the solar disc that was encircled with the cobra Wadjet.

As soon as I stepped across the threshold, the large, heavy wooden door boomed closed behind me. Her magnetic presence drew me near. An ethereal shaft of blue light illuminated her, standing there as if waiting for me with a beckoning Buddha smile. Again, I heard her voice say, "If you want my power, suckle at my breast." Standing on tiptoes beneath her, I opened my mouth and placed my lips around her stone teat. Instantly, I became a suckling lion cub, greedily pulling at my momma's nipple for nourishment. I drank until sated. I swooned and then crouched down into the fetal position at her feet, seeing myself as the sleeping cub, nuzzling at the soft underbelly of big momma cat. When my ordinary consciousness came back, I tucked a tiny fig I had plucked from Hathor's sacred Sycamore tree outside the chapel underneath her feet as an offering. It seemed as though hours has passed when I exited, but it had only been ten or fifteen minutes. I felt drunk and exhilarated at the same time. I walked around the temple grounds in deep trance and, upon returning to my room on the cruise ship, slept like a baby.

Later, Nicki gave the group advice on the journeying process. She said not to figure it out, that understanding was the booby prize. She explained that it was more important to arrive at a new level of meaning, even though it may take time for this new perspective to sink in.

"Let your subconscious take over to pull the whole process together. As you go through life you'll flash on something to crystallize awareness. Cultivate your ability to seamlessly go between the worlds. It is always there simultaneous with ordinary reality."

I felt fortified after this experience with Sekhmet, but I never got over the reeling, swooning energy that Egypt had given me, nor the feeling of being very young and innocent. Indeed, though I was a seasoned priestess, in this land I was the neophyte being nourished by the Goddess.

The following morning our wake up call was early again. We had to drive through the country on the West Bank of the Nile to get to Hathor's temple at Dendera. When we arrived, we were ushered through the gates ahead of the other tourists. We were dressed in white galabayas that had been made especially for our group for the occasion of a birthing ceremony in the temple of the Goddess of Love, dance, music, birth, and so much more. I was excited to dance in the temple of the Goddess to whom I was ordained.

We were led through a tunnel-like passageway with hieroglyphs and bas reliefs of Hathor on either side of the walls. My hands reached out, skimming the surfaces so I could glean their energies. On one of them, I kissed Hathor's bare belly button in reverence to her. When we came through that passageway, several people from our group were lined up, forming a symbolic birth canal. We were pushed down and through and then lifted out. Next, we were guided to the room with the famous circular zodiac. I found my "horus-scope," the winged centaur, Sagittarius, inscribed upon the ceiling.

I changed into a turquoise galabaya—because turquoise is the color associated with Hathor—and added accessories of gold scarves and a turquoise-beaded headdress. I climbed up to the rooftop where I was to dance Hathor for the group. The energy of the Goddess moved up into the soles of my bare feet. I mimed holding her sacred mirror of the soul, looking at myself and then out to others, showing them their reflection. As the Goddess of auspicious beauty, Hathor teaches us to see the reflection of our own beauty in her mirror and to love ourselves unconditionally.

Later that day, we visited Abydos, the temple dedicated to Osiris. It is said to be the place where Osiris's dismembered head was found. I was in wonder over the beautiful temple walls and the story of Osiris's resurrection, the birth of Horus, and his training. It was powerful and profound to see the reliefs of the Goddesses blessing him and to see the birth of the Gods on earth.

Our final excursion of the trip was a private evening visit into the Great Pyramid of Giza.

Nicki said that in our journeys, we had passed through the fire of mysteries. "In the sarcophagus, you will receive the kiss of Amun Ra and then rise up like the phoenix into the sahu body, the shining intelligence of the Ankh. Receive the transmission and come into coherence."

Now that we had been through these rites—each one of us a divine being, a neter, a part of the one God who had come to know more deeply our own divinity—Nicki suggested that we ask ourselves these questions: "What is my intention now? What is it I wish to do or become? How can these mysteries influence my future?"

Inside the King's Chamber of the Great Pyramid, the energy was so strong that I had to sit down the entire time during our ceremony. The answer I received was to compile and produce my Egyptian Goddess dances—Isis, Nepthys, Selkhet, Shesat, Sekhmet, Hathor, Neith, Ma'at, Nuit and Mut—so that others could appreciate the timeless wisdom that channels through my body. Most of these dances have only been performed at the Temple of Isis in California. Now my assignment was to share these powerful feminine qualities of the ancient Egyptian pantheon of Goddesses with the public at large. I did not know how or when I would do this, but because it was asked of me, I would have to make it happen.

When my turn came to lie in the sarcophagus, suddenly I was surrounded and permeated by wheels within wheels of counter-rotating luminescent fields. My *Merkabah* instantly activated. Sparks flew off me. Spirals of divine effulgence transported my spirit into higher dimensions. It was as if the stone coffin itself existed only to contain my physical body while my light body soared to the heavens. My whole being vibrated violently, gaining velocity as it traveled at warp speed through a portal to shoot straight up into the cosmos. Imploding and exploding at the same moment, I transformed into a star.

This was the closest to God I have ever been in my life. One day, my rightful place awaits me, so clear beyond the stars, beyond the imperishable stars…

Le'ema in Egypt dancing at Isis's Temple

Choreographic Works

2009	Mut Egyptian Vulture Goddess
2008	Enchanted Play; Emerald Green Dakini; Nut and Geb
2007	Neith; Serpent Spiral Dance; Lucy in the Sky
2006	Ma'at; Mary Magdalene
2005	Hathor; Initiation; Women of the Alabaster Jar
2004	Selkhet
2003	Seshet
2002	Isis/Nepthys; Horus
2001	Demeter & Persephone; Athena; Flying Home; In the Temple of the Silver Serpent
2000	Minoan Snake Priestess; Ancient Egyptian Pharaohnic Dance
1999	Fields of Gold; The Green Man & the Snake
1998	Ma Kali; Hathor & Horus
1997	A Dedication to Mother Theresa; Guadalupe: Path of the Broken Heart/Goddess of the Americas; Medusa; Sea Goddesses; Gypsy Love Duet
1996	Brigid; The Virgin and the Whore; The Crone's Reawakening
1995	Celtic Woman
1994	Lamia
1993	Inanna/Dance of the Seven Veils; Ma Kali
1992	Aphrodite; The Pregnant Virgin
1991	Love, Lover, Beloved

1990	Moon Goddess; Black Madonna
1989	Elohim
1988	Green Tara; Persephone Rising; Pandora's Box; Invasion of the Sextra-Terrestrial; Rescue
1987	Suite Kundalini; No Latin Lover
1986	Journey; Power of Love; What a Workout
1985	City Life
1984	(Outer Space Audition for the Boys + Mourning Mantra) x 1 = Father Sky/Mother Earth
1983	Samba
1982	A Lady Artist Alone/Self-Weaning; Priestess; Gypsy Dance; Les Follies Derriere Du Monde; The Ballad of Norma Jean
1981	The Dune Works; Doin' the Dance of Back Packing in the Big City
1980	Species Extinct
1979	When That Girl Was Walking There in the Desert...; Suite for Old Love; Smuckstick
1978	Flame
1977	Sun Blessing

Reading List

Al-Rawi, Rosina-Fawzia. *Grandmother's Secrets: The Ancient Rituals and Healing Power of Belly Dancing.* New York: Interlink Books, 2003.

Ashby, Dr. Muata Abhaya. *The Serpent Power.* Florida: Cruzian Mystic Books, 1997.

Austen, Hallie Iglehart. *The Heart of the Goddess: Art, Myth and Meditations of the World's Sacred Feminine.* Oakland: Wingbow Press, 1990

Buonaventura, Wendy. *Serpent of the Nile: Women and Dance in the Arab World.* London: Saqi Books, 1989.

Dintino, Theresa. *Ode to Minoa.* Pittsburgh: Sterling House, 1999.

Duncan, Isidora. *The Art of the Dance.* New York: Theatre Arts Books, 1969.

Ellis, Normandi. *Awakening Osiris: The Egyptian Book of the Dead.* Grand Rapids: Phanes Press, 1988.

Ellis, Normandi. *Dreams of Isis.* Illinois: Quest Books, 1995.

Ellis, Normandi. *Feasts of Light: Celebrations for the Seasons of Life.* Illinois: Quest Books, 1999.

Forrest, M. Isidora. *Offering to Isis: Knowing the Goddess Through Her Sacred Symbols.* St. Paul: Llewllyn, 2005.

Foubister, Linda. *Goddess in the Grass: Serpentine Mythology and the Great Goddess.* Victoria: Ecce Nova Editions, 2003.

Gimbutas, Marija. *Civilization of the Goddess.* New York: Harper, 1991.

Johnsen, Linda. *The Living Goddess: Reclaiming the Tradition of the Mother of the Universe.* St. Paul: Yes International Publishers, 1999.

Johnson, Buffie. *Lady of the Beasts: the Goddess and Her Sacred Animals.* Vermont: Inner Traditions International. 1994.

Johnson, Sally B. *The Cobra Goddess of Ancient Egypt.* London and New York: Kegan Paul International, 1990.

Marashinsky, Amy Sophia. *The Goddess Oracle: A Way to Wholeness through the Goddess and Ritual.* Rockport: Element Books, Inc. 1997.

Melchizedek, Drunvalo. *Serpent of Light, Beyond 2012: The Movement of the Earth's Kundalini and the Rise of the Female Light, 1949 to 2013.* San Francisco: Weiser Books, 2008.

Mini, John. *The Aztec Virgin: The Secret Mystical Tradition of Our Lady of Guadalupe.* Sausalito: Trans-Hyperborean Institute of Science, 2000.

Mookerjee, Ajit. *Kali The Feminine Force.* New York: Destiny Books, 1988.

Narby, Jeremy. *The Cosmic Serpent: DNA and the Origins of Knowledge.* New York: Putnam, 1998.

Noble, Vicki. *Motherpeace: A Way to the Goddess through Myth, Art, and Tarot.* San Francisco: Harper & Row, 1983.

Noble, Vicki. *Shakti Woman: Feeling Our Fire, Healing Our World.* Harper San Francisco, 1991.

Noble, Vicki. *Uncoiling the Snake.* San Francisco: Harper San Francisco, 1993.

Pinkham, Mark Amaru. *The Return of the Serpents of Wisdom.* Illinois: Adventures Unlimited Press, 1997.

Regula, DeTraci. *The Mysteries of Isis: Her Worship and Magic.* Minnesota: Llewellyn Publications, 1996.

Rigoglioso, Marguerite. *The Cult of Divine Birth in Ancient Greece.* New York: Palgrave Macmillan, 2009.

Robertson, Olivia. *The Call of Isis.* London: Neptune Press, 1975.

Rose, Sharron. *The Path of the Priestess: A Guidebook for Awakening the Divine Feminine.* Vermont: Inner Traditions, 2002.

Sams, Jamie and David Carson. *Medicine Cards: The Discovery of Power Through the Ways of Animals.* Santa Fe: Bear & Company, 1988.

Scully, Nicki. *Power Animal Meditations.* Vermont: Bear & Company, 1991.

Scully, Nicki. *Alchemical Healing: A Guide to Spiritual, Physical, and Transformational Medicine.* Vermont: Bear & Company, 2003.

Scully, Nicki and Star Wolf, Linda. *Shamanic Mysteries of Egypt: Awakening the Healing Power of the Heart.* Vermont: Bear & Company, 2007.

Starbird, Margaret. *The Woman with the Alabaster Jar: Mary Magdalen and the Holy Grail.* Santa Fe: Bear & Company, 1993.

Starhawk. *The Spiral Dance: A Rebirth of the Ancient Religion of the Great Goddess, 20th Anniversary Edition.* San Francisco: Harper, 1999.

Stewart, Iris. *Sacred Woman, Sacred Dance.* Vermont: Inner Traditions, 2000.

Tate, Karen. *Walking an Ancient Path: Rebirthing Goddess on Planet Earth.* Winchester, UK: O Books, 2008.

Walker, Barbara G. *The Woman's Encyclopedia of Myths and Secrets.* San Francisco: Harper and Row, 1983.

Waters, Frank. *Book of the Hopi.* New York: Penguin Books, 1978.

About the Author

Rev. Le'ema Kathleen Graham, BFA, RYT, truly expresses spirit in the body through dance as a vehicle for meditation and healing. She is a visionary sacred dancer, choreographer, ritual-maker, teacher, and minister in the temple of Isis.

Le'ema works with serpent power as snake keeper, yogini, mystic, and medicine woman. She is a Priestess Hierophant in the Fellowship of Isis, and the Temple of Isis, and is founder of Isis of the Snakes Iseum.

Internationally recognized in the Goddess Movement, she has a degree in dance/theater arts and thirty years experience on stage, television and film. Her classes and performances reveal a spiritual vision with social, political and environmental consciousness.

As a teacher Le'ema is a profound catalyst for awakening and empowering the unique personal wisdom residing within each one of us. She leads retreats and workshops internationally.

Le'ema lives in San Rafael, California with her husband Élan and son Liam, along with their Brussels Griffon dog Dobby and a tuxedo cat Moonshadow, plus four serpents: Isis, a Columbian Red Tailed Boa, Pyro, a North American Corn snake, and Nidaba and Monty, Pythons.

In 2008 GoddessWork published Le'ema's DVD titled *Snake Yoga: Sacred Feminine Wisdom*.

For more information, please visit www.goddesswork.com

Snake Yoga

Please visit www.snakeyoga.com for more info on Le'ema's *Snake Yoga: Sacred Feminine Wisdom* instructional DVD.

$24.95 plus tax and shipping

www.ingramcontent.com/pod-product-compliance
Lightning Source LLC
Chambersburg PA
CBHW031558110426
42742CB00036B/242